SPEAKER'S EDGE

WORLD CHAMPION SPEAKERS

SECRETS AND STRATEGIES FOR CONNECTING WITH ANY AUDIENCE

MARK BROWN DARREN LACROIX PATRICIA FRIPP ED TATE CRAIG VALENTINE

Soar
with
Eagles

A Publisher Driven
by Vision and Purpose
www.soarhigher.com

*Speaker's EDGE: Secrets and Strategies
for Connecting with Any Audience*

ISBN-13: 978-0-9814756-0-8
Library of Congress Control Number 2009927534

First Edition

Published by
Soar with Eagles
1200 North Mallard Lane, Rogers, AR 72756, USA
 www.soarhigher.com

Printed in the United States of America

Cover design and layout by Carrie Perrien Smith
Editing by Gregory Lay and Carrie Perrien Smith

CONTENTS

Dedication

*To our EDGE members who prove
time and time again that
these processes work*

INTRODUCTION
This Isn't Just Another Book on Presentations

Improve your public speaking skills with useful resources from four World Champions and a Hall of Fame Speaker! The five experts featured in this book represent the best of the best in the world of public speaking and presentation coaching.

They cover topics as diverse as humor, motivation, public speaking, communication skills, leadership, and personal and organizational excellence. There's no other place in the world where you will find this much skill, talent, passion, and entertainment!

How fast do you want to take your speaking to the next level?

Stop wasting time on the expensive "guessing game" trying to become a great speaker. This book provides great information and gives you a sneak peak at the fastest track to becoming a world-class speaker — the World Champions' EDGE speaker education programs.

Champions' EDGE Members receive weekly audio lessons, monthly CDs and conference

This book contains three sections focused on the objective of helping you become amazing on the platform:

- **Platform Presence.** This section is devoted to helping you create impact from the moment you step on stage until you bid goodbye to your audience.

- **Content Excellence.** At the core of every great presentation is well-written content. You'll learn the secrets of writing compelling speeches.

- **Winning Techniques.** From sales presentation tips to earning credentials and expertise, this section will help you win more often and experience success.

calls, 20 percent savings on Champ Camps and educational tools, and much more! Plus, they have a chance to network with other like-minded speakers.

Whether you have a fear of public speaking or have given presentations for years, you'll find this is not your average public speaking book and that World Champions' EDGE is not your typical public speaking resource. Both will change the way you look at presentations forever.

What do great speakers do differently? What are the biggest mistakes most presenters make? What do speakers need to know to get booked more often? Join us on the journey to train some of the best speakers of tomorrow.

Stage time,
Darren LaCroix
2001 World Champion of Public Speaking

Platform Presence

CHAPTER 1
Connecting with an Unfamiliar Audience

Immerse Yourself in Their Experience On and Off the Stage!

by Darren LaCroix

If you are a celebrity speaker earning tens of thousands of dollars per speech, you don't need any help "connecting" with your audience. You are famous. You have their attention. For the rest of us, to best serve our audiences, we need to go above and beyond to connect with them. Sometimes I speak in the Toastmasters world where I have instant credibility due to my accomplishment as the 2001 World Champion of Public Speaking. However, when I speak to a group outside of Toastmasters, no one really cares that I won the World Championship. I regularly speak to associations around the country, and they have no idea who I am other than reading my bio in the program. So, how do I connect with them?

Let's first talk about connecting using "off the stage" experience. When I first started speaking professionally, my experience was an opening act as a comedian struggling to do ten strong minutes of material. As a professional speaker, I had to be up there for an hour! To make the jump, I learned to do anything and everything I could to connect with them. I interviewed people ahead of time, read newsletters, dove into their website, and for sure, showed up early. I made it a priority to invest the extra time before I spoke at a conference to immerse myself in the experience so I would be on target with the audience when I took the stage to speak. I still incorporate many of the techniques I developed from my early days — especially when I know the audience is in a different industry than I'm used to.

Show Up Early

You want to arrive at an event early and spend as much time with attendees as you can. I live in Las Vegas and the time zone difference can make it challenging to get to an event on the east coast when I'm speaking in my area the day before. Ideally, you want to arrange to arrive at the meeting site the day before the event so you are rested and relaxed. Airline travel has many variables — weather delays, missed connections, and cancellations just to name a few. If you are scheduled to arrive just a few hours before your speaking engagement, a problem with your flight could cause you to miss the engagement altogether. That would not only let the client down, it would damage your reputation and ensure you would not get any repeat business. If you were booked by a speaker bureau, it would damage their relationship with that client as well. It would probably ensure they never considered you again.

Besides allowing you to avoid any schedule mishaps, arriving early allows you to participate in all the activities. I presume you know your topic and are an expert (or an expert in the making) on your speech topic. Although your message may be perfect for your audience, it is still our job to draw the audience in. This may be the first time they've heard your message, and some of them could be looking for reasons to disagree with your message. Arriving early and doing your homework helps you discover ways to connect your message to their lives so it seems more relevant.

Six Keys to Connecting
Your Keynote to Your Audience

Recently, I spoke for a transportation company's national safe driver awards banquet. This was an audience of 150 truck drivers and their spouses. Here are six techniques I used that can help you connect to an audience no matter how unfamiliar they are to you.

Immerse Yourself in the Experience!

Conferences can range from a small meeting with a few presentations all the way to a huge program that features activities, games, trade shows, and gala evenings. Whatever the attendees are doing, immerse yourself in their experience, and observe what they do. Some of the time invested may feel wasted, but remember, we are looking for just a couple gems to anchor our message to. If there is a trade show, walk it. If there are sessions before yours, sit in on them. If there are fun activities, have fun!

The transportation company trade show had a million-dollar driving simulator. It is designed to train and test divers on how to handle adverse conditions. For this conference, it was used as a fun, hands-on activity. Though most of the drivers were men, many of the wives attending jumped in and tried the simulator. They were having fun. I watched and observed some of them, and made sure I learned the names of the people I saw drive. Later during my keynote, I had fun with it.

The other added bonus this gives you is that when these people see you up there speaking, you can see in their faces that they are thinking, "Hey, that's the guy we saw in the simulator!" Once that happens, I now have created some friends in the audience. It always helps having friendly faces who are connected to you at a deeper level.

Ask Questions and SHUT UP!

It's not about you! Though I may be the keynote speaker, I don't care if they like me. I care that they get my message. The same is true when I am doing my on-site research. You only have a limited time to learn about them. If you are talking about yourself, you are decreasing the time you will learn about them.

I went into the simulator and did a lot of eavesdropping. When it was my turn, I asked Bob and Randy (the simulator operators) some questions. Then I did the best thing I could — I shut up and took notes.

Recognize the People They are Honoring

This particular event was an awards banquet. Whoever they are honoring, I knew I must at least mention them as well. I also made sure that I honored the past national champions. How can you honor them? Sometimes mentioning them is enough. You might want to give them a free copy of your book or audio CD. Sometimes sharing one of their stories is effective. Your technique may vary from speech to speech. You are the keynoter — you decide what is appropriate. Do not spend too much time on it though. Be real, be quick, and make it fun if you can.

Recognize the People Who Made
Their Conference a Memorable Experience

As speakers, we often get much of the glory and have most of the fun at a conference. There are many people who put in hours and hours of effort to make the conference flow smoothly. They rarely get the recognition they deserve. Having a keynote speaker recognize them goes a long way, and it's just the right thing to do. Depending on the situation, I make a point to give them a free copy of my book too. It means a great deal to them. I made sure I recognized Randy and Bob.

Always Play Up to Your Audience

Johnny Carson (former *Tonight Show* host) was asked in an interview, "Why do you think you were so successful?" He paused, gathered his thoughts, and said, "I always played up to my audiences."

In this day and age when it is getting tougher to entertain, many comedians are resorting to negativity and cutting people down. Johnny always respected the audience's intelligence. He always put himself down, not the audience.

You must keep this in mind when you are the outsider. Even when I do my famous "gestures" routine, I always prompt my helpers that they can do what they want to me, but I cannot put them in a tough situation. They are "one of them (audience members)." If I was mean or negative to my helper, my audience would turn on me. If my helper embarrasses me, the audience loves it because the helper is an extension of them.

Always Recognize Guests, But ...

If you are a Toastmaster, I'm not talking about saying, "Mr. Toastmaster, fellow Toastmasters, and guests." I'm talking about going much deeper than that and recognizing one "specific" person — an actual observation goes much deeper to create a connection. It does not have to take much time, but should be "real." All acknowledgements should be strategically placed in your speech. At this particular keynote, I recognized people before I even started the presentation. For example, I said, "Before I get started, where is Ms. Johnson. Wow, are you okay? I was there in the driving simulation when you accidentally drove off the bridge. I was worried about you!" I will usually pick two to three people to acknowledge before I actually start my presentation.

Keynote audiences vary greatly. Evaluate each one on a case-by-case basis. Following these six guidelines will give you a framework to find deeper ways to connect as you make it a habit to immerse yourself in the attendee experience.

The Emotional Tap: The Fastest Way to Connect

Now let's look at using common on-stage experience from an audience view point. What have they all witnessed happening on stage?

When you get advice from someone who's a true master of his craft, does it make sense to follow it, even if the advice is inconvenient?

One of the most profound bits of advice I received early in my career was from one of my comedy mentors, Vinnie Favorito. He said, "Darren, you must always show up early and watch the whole show. You need to know what everyone in front of you is doing on stage."

There are several reasons for this. If the presenter (or comedian) before us speaks about the same subject, it's our responsibility to know that. This differs from the previous section because now we are talking about familiarizing ourselves with other presenters versus other experiences at a conference off the stage.

It's also a huge opportunity to set ourselves apart and connect. If we can "tap into" what others said before us, audience members will know that our presentation isn't "canned." It separates us from other speakers (especially if you are a competitive speaker). One word of caution: don't stretch to include something if it's not a direct tie-in. It must be a sincere connection to what you're talking about.

If a presenter before me has a profound thought or funny line that the audience loves, it becomes an emotionally charged line or phrase. I always look to see if there is a way for me to tap into the emotion — it's something that's only good that day with that audience. Being present in that moment with them is what makes it so special. When we can tap into an emotionally charged phrase, it allows us to create a quick and powerful connection with the audience.

I believe in this so much that I changed my travel plans to arrive at a Washington DC convention a day early one year. Fellow World Champion of Public Speaking Ed Tate was doing the opening keynote, and I was scheduled to speak the next day. Although I had to leave our Champions' EDGE Summit early (and still did not get to DC until 1:00 a.m.), it was worth it. Ed's keynote was the only general session that was seen by the entire audience. Hence, it is the only speaker they will all have in common before I take the stage. It was definitely worth it!

Here's an example from the comedy stage. People are always asking me if I still do stand-up comedy. The answer over the past year has been "nope." Well, that changed recently. I was offered a guest spot at the LA Comedy Club in Las Vegas. I couldn't turn down the "stage time."

I was nervous, because that is a very different world from what I'm now used to as a speaker. I took Vinnie Favorito's advice and watched intently as the first comic took the stage. He did a series of "bald" jokes that worked very well (if the jokes had bombed, I would've taken a different approach).

I had laughs within seconds of taking the stage by tying into that concept. You should look at everything that happens on the stage before you as a setup for what you're going to do.

Want to connect fast? Show up early, watch the other speakers, and see if you can emotionally tap into their good moments. Take Vinnie's advice too!

Halfway through Your Presentation, You Realize This is Not Working!

You've prepared your presentation, you know your subject, and you have studied your audience. You have the presentation internalized. As you progress through it, you have a bad feeling that starts to grow. You're halfway through, and you hear a little voice in your head that says, "This is not working!" What do you do?

That was the exact question I got from one of my corporate coaching clients. His presentation was a "pitch" for a $150,000 per month contract. It was an extremely important presentation for him and his company. I took a minute to really think about it. Then, I remembered an amazing transformation that I experienced long ago during a comedy show.

Three of the top stand-up headliners were working a show together in Worcester, Massachusetts. There happened to be another major event in the main room, so they had to move the comedy show. Picture yourself in the audience that night — one of 115 people in a hotel basement. It was definitely not the best situation — low ceilings, a warm room, and a column in the middle of the floor that obstructed the view for many of the audience members.

The first comedian was experienced and very talented. However, when he took the stage, he only received mild laughter. He continued to follow his routine and didn't waver. The second comedian also delivered his usual routine — with the same unimpressive result.

The last comedian, Vinnie Favorito, took the stage, and started with his planned routine. He was about three minutes into it when he stopped. He put the microphone down, pulled up a stool, and said, "Guys, what's the matter? What's going on?" Vinnie changed gears and abandoned the original plan that he always used — the plan that almost always worked for him.

He realized one crucial thing. The original plan will only work when you're connected with the audience. Sometimes a connection is easy to make. On other occasions — like this — it's not.

I was just amazed at how Vinnie stopped his flow and confidently changed directions. If he had kept going, he would have suffered the same mediocre laughs that the other comedians received.

If you find yourself in the middle of a presentation and it's not working, stop. Talk to them. Check in. It's perfectly legal to ask the audience where they are and what's wrong. It takes a true professional to do that.

By checking in, I mean literally put down your notes, darken the projector screen, step forward, and separate yourself emotionally and physically from what you were doing. It gets the audience's attention and helps engage them right away. They feel the change, and can tell it was not planned. You might instantly gain a connection. If you don't gain that connection right away, I promise, checking in will be a huge step toward creating one!

How did it turn out that night in a stuffy basement? Amazing! Vinnie Favorito took a tough audience and completely turned them around. Will it work every time? That's hard to say — it depends on many factors. However, if it is not working the way it is going, please change something!

When I told my corporate client the story about Vinnie's adjustment, he didn't see what a comedian's strategy had to do with his sales presentation at first. But it didn't take him long to realize that it was about getting the focus off of himself and onto his audience.

When he learned to let go of his prepared presentation and simply ask his customers what was going on in their thoughts, he found a way to get the audience connection he needed. Witnessing a master like Vinnie perform under difficult circumstances has taught me a great deal. The next time you look at your audience and notice "this isn't working," what will you do?

Final Thoughts

Creating audience connection is one of the most powerful ways to earn a place in the memory of the audience. Being memorable (in a good way) increases the chances of being invited to speak again. It's possible to create the connection in even the toughest presentations. By doing your homework on the organization, showing up early, and getting involved with the experience will give you the opportunity to engage your audience when it really counts — when you are on the stage.

World Champions' EDGE Testimonial

 *"I've just returned from Finland where I was representing the United Kingdom in the European Finals of the JCI (Junior Chamber International) Public Speaking World Championship, and I won! I will now go forward to compete in the World Finals in Delhi, India. The tips and techniques I picked up from your Champ Camps played a HUGE part in helping me put together and deliver a winning speech. Thank you so much!"*

Simon Bucknall, London, England

World Champions' EDGE Testimonial

"Since I have joined the EDGE, I can honestly say that I have grown as a speaker. The information that is imparted to us every month is invaluable. I have used the many tips and techniques provided by the monthly EDGEucational CD and Ask the Champs coaching calls and have received fabulous feedback. The ability to connect with the Champs and Ms. Fripp and other speakers is the icing on the cake."

Marilyn Latchford
Pickering, Ontario, Canada

CHAPTER 2
Internalize Not Memorize
Get Your Presentation out of Your Head and into Your Heart

by Ed Tate

" Barack! Feel — don't think! Get out of your head. You're over-thinking." These are the words of the wife of a young senator from Illinois — today you know him as President Obama. Early in the campaign, he was on a conference call with his top advisors brainstorming the finer points of his position for an upcoming debate. Michelle Obama was listening in and finally could not take it anymore.

"Don't get caught up in the weeds. Be visceral! Use your heart and your head." What Mrs. Obama was advising her husband to do was to use his gut and to get out of his head.

Ever have an experience where you were caught overthinking? How did that work out for you? Have you given a presentation that was all "head" and no "heart"? Perhaps it was loaded with Abstract-Speak™ — techno-jargon such as facts, figures, data, and jargon — and made absolutely no impact on your audience at all. It's easy to get so focused on facts that you can forget to focus and connect with your audience.

Michelle Obama was concerned by her husband's debate performances where he had been tripped up by his rivals early in the campaign. Are you tripping up your own presentations by being "in your head" too much? Are you *memorizing* rather than *internalizing*?

Internalizing means that you own the material and it's a part of you — it's in your head and your heart. It's visceral. It's in your gut. As a result, you come across as real, authentic, and genuine. And if a speaker as experienced and talented as Barack Obama can get tripped up by being in his head, it can happen to the rest of us as well.

I have two coaching clients with excellent content, but their delivery was stuck in their heads — they were memorizing rather than internalizing. The first client sent me a copy of his speech. It was well written and funny, and it had many brilliant insights. I could not wait to see his DVD performance, but I was disappointed after I watched it. This very talented, outgoing, and energetic presenter was surprisingly stiff and uninspiring — he was in his head. It was as if he were someone else someplace else. He was not engaged with the audience.

My second coaching client is an executive of a major information technology company. He too is very talented. When I saw his DVD, initially, I was very impressed. He started strong, told stories about audience members and had two funny one-liners. Then, he disconnected from the audience. He started rattling off, facts, figures, data, and jargon — Abstract-Speak. While it is useful, information like that is not memorable. I had to play the last fifteen minutes of the presentation repeatedly to a recall the message. He was in his head. The audience just happened to be there.

I'm no exception to this affliction. I was asked to audition for a speaking/ training company. It was a rare opportunity, so I decided to compete. I made it to the finals. However, I did not make the final cut. Imagine someone who is a World Champion of Public Speaking and a Certified Speaking Professional losing? The feedback was overwhelming and unanimous: "Ed was too much in his head." I was not engaged with the audience. I was so focused on memorizing the material that I forgot the most important thing — to focus on the audience. I was in my head — not my heart or my gut.

So what can we do about it? The good news is this is easy to correct. Here are seven suggestions for getting "out of your head."

7.5 Suggestions for Getting Out of Your Head

1. **Closet envy.** And no, it's not what you think. This is a term coined by Darren LaCroix, the 2001 Toastmasters World Champion of Public Speaking. Darren has the recordings of every presentation he has ever done stored in his closet. Record every presentation you make — your

rehearsals and your final presentation. Here is what you are looking for when you listen to those:

- Robotically citing jargon, facts, stats, or abstractions
- Trying to remember something
- Looking at the ceiling or the floor for long periods of time
- Taking your eyes away from the audience

2. **Use notes.** It's okay to use notes. If you forget or do not know your material well, it's better to have them available. Here are some tips for making them useful.

   - Double-space the text and use a large font (14-point font or larger).
   - Use different colored highlighters or post-it notes to draw attention to key points.
   - On the podium, lectern, or table, always display two pages at a time. It makes it easier to find your place.
   - Rehearse using your notes. Practice this routine: pause, find your place, make eye contact, and continue.
   - Be audience-centered rather than speaker-centered. Memorizing your speech makes you look good (speaker-centered), but it doesn't necessarily serve your audience. Choose to be audience-centered.

3. **Focus on the connection, rather than the content.** The biggest mistake that most presenters make is thinking that their content is the most important part of their presentation. They spend all of their preparation focusing on content and zero time on audience connection. The most important part of your presentation is how you will connect your content with each specific audience. Focus on the connection with the audience. Here are a few connection tips for pre-session interviews.

   - Interview five attendees before your presentation. Ask questions about successes and challenges the organization is experiencing.
   - Interview leaders in the organization, and get their perspective on the economy, industry, and competition.
   - Study websites (specifically the About Us and History links), newsletters, articles, and annual reports.
   - Google them. Use the Internet to find anything you may have missed.
   - For more connection tips, check out *Connect with Any Audience: How to Read and React to People in Front of You!* (www.worldchampionresources.com)

4. **Be conversational rather than presentational.** When you are with your family and friends, do you have conversations or presentations?

Hopefully you are having conversations. Having a conversation with your audience will help you connect with them and engage them in your presentation.

5. **Know your purpose and focus on what educator and professional speaker Pam Gordon calls the KFD®** — what do you want people to know, feel, or do?

6. **Focus on the core message.** If you only had one minute and could tell them one thing, what would that be? In my award-winning speech, "Tate's Rules on Bullies," the core message is this: "Violence is not the answer. The greatest weapon you have for solving your problems is your mind. Thinking through your problems is the answer."

7. **Trust yourself.** Trust your talent. You have everything you need right now to be an outstanding presenter. Being in your head comes from the fear of forgetting a part of your message and not trusting yourself.

7.5. **Get Coaching.** Here is a bonus technique. The best golfer in the world, Tiger Woods, has a coach. If coaching works for him in his avocation, it will work for you too.

Final Thoughts

Even seasoned presenters get stuck in their head. It happens to everyone. However, the right amount of preparation and using the 7.5 Strategies for Getting out of Your Head can help you avoid this embarrassing situation. By internalizing rather than memorizing your next presentation, you will come across as persuasive, professional, and positive.

World Champions' EDGE Testimonial

"Exactly four months ago, I wrote Darren LaCroix an e-mail asking to be coached by him for the sole reason that I was the only aspiring Toastmasters World Champion from the Ukraine on the block — this was what I thought.

Hi, my name is Andriy Spivak twice-tried-never-made-it Public Speaking Champ of Ukraine.

To my surprise, he instantly replied pointing me to the EDGE for starters!

Boy, how humiliated was I discovering my true dimension against the scale of the Champs! Wow, how exciting it is to be inspired by them all along the thorny way to speaking and writing excellence!

Four months of sponging it off in a single hope of creating a perfect Andriy-tailored speech, topic, or joke, and enjoying the process every step of the way!"

Andriy Spivak, Kiyv, Ukraine

World Champions' EDGE Testimonial

 *"I met Darren LaCroix in November 1996 at a Toastmasters district conference. He twisted my arm and got me to join the EDGE — best decision I ever made. I was serious about becoming a professional speaker and about the Toastmasters International World Championship of Public Speaking. With a lot of hard work and some terrific advice from all the Champs, I was able to progress much faster than anticipated. I got to spend two days in Craig Valentine's living room getting some phenomenal feedback on my writing and delivery. In August 2008, I had the honor of representing my Toastmasters club, district, and region at the TI World Championship of Public Speaking competition. The EDGE provided me with every opportunity to succeed. It will do the same for you."*

Martin Presse, WCPS Finalist 2008
Alberta, Canada

CHAPTER 3
Unveiling the Magic for Being a More Effective Speaker

by Patricia Fripp

Part of the magic of the top speakers in the world isn't magic at all — it's technique, knowledge, skill, and preparation. This chapter will provide insider secrets for making sure your audience connects with your message the way you meant it and that they perceive you as the professional that you are.

How Our Audience Members Learn

We learn by what we see, hear, and experience; vicariously; on reflection; and by teaching others. The way our audience members learn affects the effectiveness of our message.

When your audience is small and you know the individual learning preferences, you can deliver your message in a way that meets their needs. However, it is impossible to know the learning preferences of all the individuals as your audiences grow larger — and they will grow if you are serious about building your speaking skills. This means that you must craft your message so that it meets the needs of any type of learner in your audience.

As you study how others learn, consider all the ways you learn and how it can create a richer learning experience as you develop your speaking skills. Let's explore the ways we can learn.

Learning by What You See

From now on, when you are listening and observing a great speaker, a member of a Toastmasters Club, or perhaps a business speech or sales presentation, look at it with fresh eyes. Observe how the speakers move around the front of the room or the stage, and if you arrive early, how they act in preparation.

At the Fripp Speaking Schools, I often ask, "What did you see that will help you become a more effective speaker before we even started?" I frequently hear comments like, "You were set up and organized before we arrived," or "You interacted with the group."

A couple of years ago, I was hired to deliver a one-day presentation skills training for a group of twenty engineers, scientists, and astronauts. We met for a 7:00 a.m. continental breakfast to get ready for the 7:30 a.m. start. They were sitting in their seats eating, and I made a point to introduce myself to each person and shake their hand. After my introduction, I opened by saying, "What have you already learned that would make you a more effective speaker before we officially started?"

Being an intelligent group, they all shouted out at the same time. "You went around and met everyone before you started." I said, "That is the point — we are rarely nervous of one individual. We're only nervous when they become an audience or a committee." Letting my audience reinforce what they see helped them internalize the message.

There's a lot you can learn that will make you more effective by what you see. For convention speakers, your performance actually starts when you're at the airport baggage claim. How you interact with other passengers and act when you're on the shuttle bus to the hotel leaves an impression with people who are probably going to be in your audience.

Learning by What You Hear

People can certainly learn by what they hear from the content of the speech. They can also learn by studying the speaker's vocal variety. Even a pause can give the audience members a chance to reflect on what they have heard a speaker say. Few speakers understand the importance of the pause and are comfortable with silence. When we speak so that the message will be remembered and repeated, the appropriate pauses can punctuate our most important points.

Learning by What You Experience

Experienced speakers understand that their message is not only heard — it is experienced. The richer the experience, the more impactful the message and the more memorable the program. As you study experienced speakers, you'll learn new ideas and techniques you'll want to try for yourself. Here is a word of warning: don't try six new techniques in one presentation. It will be too much and confuse you. Just take perhaps one technique at a time to incorporate in your own presentation.

Perhaps you're going to make better eye contact on silence. Or you're going to pause longer. Maybe you're going to add more creative gestures. Whatever new technique that you decide to incorporate, record your presentation for evaluation. As you listen to it later, reflect on what you learned from the experience of incorporating the new ideas.

Learning Vicariously

Speaking more often will sharpen your speaking skills, but you will find that you can learn from participating in group coaching sessions as part of a speaking school when someone coaches another speaker. You'll find you can learn a great deal at a Toastmasters Club where the speeches are evaluated. Do you notice we all have to master the same techniques? When watching someone else being coached, it is easier to observe in them what you intellectually understand but have not internally mastered. By learning vicariously, you benefit in a way that is too close to home when you are "in the hot seat."

Learning from Reflection

We've often heard, "There's the speech that you plan to give, the speech you gave, and the speech you wish you'd given." Whenever you finish a talk, reflect on the experience. Do an "after-action analysis." Always start with what you did right. What did you do superbly well that you should repeat? Your future success will come from building on your past success.

Once you've reflected on your successes in the speech, look for ways to improve it. Ask yourself, "If I were giving the speech again, what could I improve?

The Best Way to Learn — by Teaching Someone Else

The best way to learn is to teach somebody else. Whenever you learn something new, find a chance to teach others what you just learned. Take the best ideas and — using the handout or workbook — explain them to somebody else. You could explain it to your spouse at dinner, to your team in a staff meeting, or to members at your Toastmasters Club. As you teach somebody else what you've learned, it also reinforces and improves your speaking skills.

Engage Your Audience

As an executive speech coach, I am frequently asked, "What is the best way to engage an audience?" This is the advice I give attendees at my speaking schools: "The best way is to be prepared, personable, polished, practical, and profound."

Prepared

Preparation is a powerful first step in engaging your audience members. Do your homework on the organization before you get there. Your research will help you easily customize your program to the needs and interests of the attendees. You will be perceived as more interesting if you are interested. You engage your audience when it is obvious you have attempted to include THEM into the message. To make that happen, you will need to ask some important questions.

Some of the answers to your research questions can be found on the Internet in articles about the organization or industry or on the organization's website. For others, you'll need to interview key members of the organization.

Here are the key areas to research:

- Who you are speaking to? Why are they there?
- What part of the agenda will you support?
- What is the purpose of the meeting?
- What are the expected outcomes of your contribution?
- Is there a theme for the meeting?
- What is the state of their industry?
- What is the organization proud of?

- What are their challenges?
- What is a typical day in the life of the audience members?
- Can you interview a few people ahead of time who will be in the audience and find "sound bite" quotes?

Personable

Your connection with the audience begins long before the engagement. If you want to engage the audience, the first step is to be engaged in the organization. The meeting organizer will be your point of contact and your job is to make her look like a hero. A key part of how happy she will be with you will be determined with how personable she finds you to be. How you act OFF the platform is every bit as important as how you act ON the platform. Here are a few tips for being personable.

- Before the event, be responsive, easy to deal with, and meet all the organizer's deadlines.
- During the event, don't demand, change the equipment requested, or act like a celebrity.
- Before your speech, meet, shake hands, chat with attendees, and be visible and involved for at least part of the meeting.

Polished

Giving a presentation is not about being perfect as much as it is about being personable. However, your audience will expect you to know your content and have practiced your presentation. Even if you use an outline, do not be so tied to your notes that you have to read it. Knowing your content well will allow you to maintain eye contact with the audience because you won't have to look down at your notes too much.

Practical but Profound

Be sure your information is interesting and has a logical application to the audience. Your pre-program research should provide clues on what your audience needs to know about your topic. Make sure you adapt your delivery to their needs. Even the brilliant-sounding ideas that are not specific and relevant enough to the audience will be useless. Conversely, simple universal concepts are not necessarily simplistic. Your observations and recommendations based on your experience and wisdom can make them profound.

Don't Speak Too Quickly in Front of Your Audience

You're charged with energy and maybe a bit nervous. Too often, this can translate into talking too fast. It might even result in a rise in voice pitch until the best-intentioned speaker sounds like Minnie Mouse. Worse yet, it can affect how the audience responds to your message.

So how do you know if your pace is right? Pay attention to audience feedback. If one person reports a problem with understanding you, this may be an individual perception or opinion. If several do, it's time to time yourself as you deliver your program.

Try this test: record a casual conversation with a friend. Then compare the number of words per minute to a recording of one of your recent speaking presentations. Do you always speak quickly or just when you're giving a speech? Did you deliberately speed up your presentation to meet some time constraint? If so, were you trying to include too much material? That's a sign that you should cut some information to make the rest more effective. Remember, the audience does not know exactly what you intended to say so they won't know what you left out!

If you decide you need to slow down your delivery, start before you even hit the stage. When you are putting together your remarks, think about logical places to slow down. It's okay to speak quickly as long as you leave yourself room for pauses and silence. This is when you think and the audience digests what they heard. After all, you want your audience to remember and be able to repeat your message.

The faster you talk, the longer your pauses should be. Give the audience time to digest what you've just said. If you say something really profound or suggest something like, "Consider the proposal in front of you," you are asking the audience to think. Give them time to do so.

Finally, here's an excellent slow-down exercise. Practice reading your speech aloud. Pause for one second at a comma, two seconds at the end of a sentence, and three seconds after a paragraph. (You can count the seconds the same way you did as a child, saying "one-Mississippi, two-Mississippi, three-Mississippi" silently to yourself.) Then breathe ... and smile! Go speak like the champion you are or will soon be!

Build Emotional Connection through Eye Contact

Eye contact is an important way to emotionally connect with an audience of any size. Generally speaking, the longer the eye contact is maintained between two people, the greater the intimacy that is developed. Eye contact has been shown to be a significant factor in the persuasion process.

So how long should you maintain eye contact with a person? In a business, sales, or speech situation, look at members of your audience long enough to convey a single thought, phrase, or idea. Practice across the dinner table with your family or friends. Whether it's a boardroom table or the dinner table, make sure you share eye contact with everyone.

Others rarely interrupt two people engaged in a conversation if they have consistent eye contact. Through observing eye contact, others — at least thoughtful ones — can tell if it is okay to join in the conversation.

Eye contact can have a powerful effect on how people perceive you. The more eye contact you can maintain, the more self-esteem people perceive you have. Eye contact is also an important way to build an emotional bond and likability. Self-esteem and likability gives you an edge in business. It's the sign of a winner and people want to do business with a winner.

Our eyes are an important part of the delivery of our message. The clearer your eyes, the more attractive you will be perceived. If you wear sunglasses, get ready to take them off because people want to see your eyes. Take care to avoid or soothe tired or bloodshot eyes because your business contacts and audience members will notice.

Your eyes react to the emotion in a conversation and give you an idea of how someone is feeling about what you are saying. Pupils enlarge when people are talking about things that bring them joy or happiness. They often contract when discussing issues that bring them sadness. In a conversation at a networking or social event, I always like to ask questions of interest to my conversation partner. It helps add to their "I enjoyed meeting that person" feeling and helps create an emotional bond so they'll remember me when it comes time to do business.

Getting Over the Jitters Before You Speak

You're waiting your turn to make a speech, when suddenly you realize that your stomach is doing strange things, and your mind is rapidly going blank. How do you handle this critical time period?

People ask me this question in all my speaking classes, but there is no single answer. You need to anticipate your speech mentally, physically, and logistically.

Prepare Mentally

Start by understanding that you'll spend a lot more time preparing than you will speaking. As a general rule, invest three hours of preparation for a half-hour speech, a six-to-one ratio. When you've become a highly experienced speaker, you may be able to cut preparation time considerably in some cases, but until then, don't skimp.

Part of your preparation will be to memorize your opening and closing — three or four sentences each. Even if you cover your key points from notes, knowing your opening and closing by heart lets you start and end fluently, connecting with your audience when you are most nervous.

Prepare Logistically

Go to the room where you'll be speaking as early as possible so you can get comfortable in the environment. If you will be speaking from a stage, go early in the morning when no one is there, and make friends with the stage. Walk around in the area where you will be speaking, so your first time there is not when you deliver your talk. Then, during your presentation, you can concentrate on your audience instead of worrying about your environment.

Prepare Physically

A wonderful preparation technique for small meetings is to shake hands and make eye contact with everybody beforehand. For larger meetings, meet and shake hands with people sitting in the front row at least and meet some of the people as they are coming in the door. Connect with them personally so they'll be rooting for your success. As speakers, we are rarely nervous about meeting individuals. Often, we are most nervous when faced with the thought of an audience. Once you've met the audience or at least some of the individuals, they become less scary.

It's totally natural to be nervous. Try this acting technique. Find a private spot, and wave your hands in the air. Relax your jaw, and shake your head from side to side. Then shake your legs one at a time. Physically shake the tension out of your body.

Try not to sit down too much while you're waiting to speak. If you're scheduled to go on an hour into the program, try to sit in the back of the room so that you can stand up occasionally. It is hard to jump up and be dynamic when you've been relaxed in a chair for an hour. Comedian Robin Williams is well known for doing jumping jacks to raise his energy level before going on stage. Sitting in the back also gives you easy access to the bathroom and drinking fountain. There's nothing worse than being stuck down front and being distracted by urgent bodily sensations.

Physical Preparation: Warm Up and Relax Your Body and Face

When you are on the platform, all eyes are on you. Warming up your body and face will help you look more natural and professional, and you will feel more relaxed. With large audiences when your talk is projected using I-MAG (image magnification), the audience will be looking at you more like they do at the movies — bigger than life. Here are some simple techniques used by actors.

1. Stand on one leg and shake the other. Hold on to a chair if you need to. When you put your foot back on the ground, it's going to feel lighter than the other one. Now, switch legs and shake. You want your energy to go through the floor and out of your head. This sounds quite cosmic; it isn't. It's a practical technique used by actors.

2. Shake your hands fast. Hold them above your head, bending at the wrist and elbow, and then bring your hands back down. This will make your hand movements more natural. Pretend to "conduct" for a few moments.

3. Warm up your face muscles by chewing in a highly exaggerated way.

4. Do shoulder and neck rolls.

5. Warm up your eyes by looking at an imaginary clock. Look at 12:00, move them to 3:00, then down to 6:00, up to 9:00, and then 12:00 again. After doing this three times, reverse the direction and repeat the steps three more times.

All of these exercises serve to warm up and relax you. Those exaggerated movements make it easier for your movements to flow more naturally. Now you can concentrate on your message and connecting to the audience.

Seven Timely Tips for Pre-Presentation Preparation

The big day has come. You are ready to deliver your presentation. To guarantee your success, there are still a few final steps to take before you face your audience.

- **Arrive early to check out the logistics of the room in which you will be speaking.** Is there a platform? If so, where is it located? Where will you stand when you are introduced? How will you reach the lectern? Is the audience close enough to where you will be speaking to build intimacy? Will the light be pointed on you if you will not be using the lectern? Proper lighting will allow you to more effectively communicate with your audience. Research shows if you put the sound *up* and the lights *down*, audience members will think they can't hear!

- **Make friends with the stage.** When the room is empty, walk on the stage, block your presentation (blocking is the process an actor uses to determine the right place on the stage for delivering particular parts of the content), and then go through the outline of your talk. Imagine an enthusiastic response.

- **Take a clock.** Make sure it is large enough see from a distance. A large kitchen clock usually works well.

- **Check out the microphone.** Do you have your preferred microphone — handheld, lavaliere (lapel), or lectern? Learn how to turn the microphone off and on and how to smoothly remove it from the stand. Practice talking into it (the proper placement is chin level for a handheld microphone). Ask someone to walk around and check to make sure you can be heard from all parts of the room.

- **Check out the audiovisual equipment.** If you are using a PowerPoint® presentation with a projector, make sure the equipment is working well. Are your PowerPoint slides in the right sequence? I recommend using a remote control to advance your slides so you can move around the audience without being chained to your computer. Practice using the B-key on your keyboard to turn the slide to black when you are not addressing what is on the screen. This will ensure the audience will pay attention to you instead of staring at the screen.

- **Connect with the organizer or emcee.** Be clear about who will introduce you and where you'll be waiting. Determine whether you will you enter the stage from the wings or come up from the floor.

- **Provide the organizer or emcee a pre-written introduction in advance.** Carry another copy with you. Format it in at least 18-point type with each line as a bullet point. Bullets are easier to read than paragraphs. Be sure your introducer knows how to pronounce your name correctly.

Final Thoughts

Now you know some of the secrets of some of the most experienced speakers. Understanding all the ways your audience members learn will help you adapt your message to the greatest number possible. Once you've done that, making sure you are prepared, personable, polished, practical, and profound will make sure you achieve impact. And with the last-minute preparation tips, all you have left to do is to stand up straight, smile, breathe, and be dynamic!

World Champions' EDGE Testimonial

 *'Being a Champions' EDGE member from its birth, the benefits have been unbelievable for me as a presentation skills instructor, coach, and keynote speaker. I have used the EDGE discount to attend many Champ Camps, invest in the many of the incredible World Champion Resources, and receive outstanding weekly EDGEucational lessons. My enhanced knowledge and skills have inspired teaching topics for my workshops and my monthly newsletters. I'm collecting all the newsletter information to incorporate into a speaking skills book. Thank you for helping establish credibility and expertise in this new career path!*

Kathryn MacKenzie BA, MEd,
Keynote Speaker, Professor,
Presentation Skills Trainer and Coach
Toronto, Ontario, Canada

CHAPTER 4

How to Lose an Audience in Ten Ways

It Worked on the "Silver Screen," So Let's Apply This Reverse Formula to Our Presentations

by Mark Brown

I enjoy films and often join my wife, Andrea — popcorn and iced tea in hand — to watch a "chick flick." The term refers to movies with strong emotional content and an emphasis on relationships that appeal to a female audience. Some time ago, we sat down to watch a film of that genre called *How to Lose a Guy in Ten Days*, starring American movie actors Kate Hudson and Matthew McConaughey.

The title intrigued me because the concept of losing something — besides extra body weight — seems contrary to conventional wisdom. We usually focus on what we can get, not what we can lose. My fellow World Champions of Public Speaking and I invest a lot of time coaching aspiring speakers on how to win an audience, but it occurred to me that the concept of losing can be applied to public speaking. There are myriad mistakes that speakers make that alienate listeners — sometimes actually sending them right out the door!

Understanding those mistakes can spare you from the discomfort, pain, and embarrassment of losing your audience. To that end, I offer five dos and five don'ts to explain how to lose an audience in ten ways.

Do Employ the Wisdom of the
Great Philosopher Confuse-Us

No, not Confucius — *Confuse-Us!* Your goal is to do all you can to confuse your audience. You can achieve this by saying things that make no sense. Disconnected statements that bemuse and befuddle your audience will put you on track towards confusion.

Contradictory statements and conflicting details are very helpful, including unverified statistics that don't support you message. For instance, "You can win 90 percent of the battle by getting the first 40 percent of the work done before your deadline. The other 60 percent, when completed, will account for the remaining 10 percent. It's really quite simple!"

When you can leave your audience scratching their heads, then you've accomplished this goal.

Do Meander

Like a babbling brook or a blathering idiot, take your audience through a labyrinth of confusing turns. Use lefts and rights, ups and downs; go north, south, east, and west. It's helpful to start out on a given path with a clear objective and then — with no warning — digress.

Be sure the point of digression is totally unrelated to your topic. If you're talking about customer service, just turn a sharp corner and begin a discourse on the importance of high-occupancy vehicle lanes in large metropolitan areas.

You get extra points when you make the irrelevant turn without completing your original point. In fact, NEVER return to your original point. Take the audience hither, thither, and yon — with the emphasis on YON.

A combination of the wisdom of Confuse-Us and a pointless meander will drive away most audiences. But if you've still got a few people left in their seats, don't worry. There are plenty of losing techniques ahead.

Do Dizzy Them with Obscure References
and Mind-Numbing Minutiae

Give the audience more statistics than a team of thirty accountants could handle. As with meandering, ensure that your information has no relevance to your topic.

I liken this technique to color commentators at a sporting event who feel the need to fill air time with statistics that precious few people would ever want to know.

For example, if you're using sports as a metaphor for life, you could say, "Life has many opportunities, but timing plays a vital role in success. Fred, a baseball player, was confident that the stars had aligned for him when he was up to bat in a crucial game last week. He knew that he had a .376 batting average when batting left-handed on a Tuesday night after 6:17 p.m. when facing a right-hander from the Midwestern states after a rain delay with men on first and third in the bottom half of the fourth or seventh innings. And that's where this company is today!"

Try this any time you want to leave your audience scratching their heads in disbelief!

Do Speak in a Monotone

Your vocal inflection and intonation must never vary. Your speaking rate and the pitch of your voice should be inflexible. Give no hint of excitement or emotion at any time. This technique is especially effective when you're conducting a multi-day seminar program in a stuffy room.

If you happen to (accidentally) tell a story, avoid any change in your voice that might distinguish the characters. Everyone must sound exactly the same — as will the sounds of snoring in your audience.

Do Pontificate

It's important to be self-serving and egotistical with your audience. Let them know — in no uncertain terms — that YOU are the expert, YOU have all the answers, YOU are the solution to all their problems, and they know nothing.

They must understand that YOU are the person on the platform with the microphone, and they are extremely fortunate to get the benefit of your vast experience and unsurpassed wisdom. Remind them by your words and manner that they are pathetically benighted and should be thankful that you are there to enlighten them. Okay, those are five things you can *do* to lose an audience. Now let's examine what you *don't* want to do so that you won't accidentally win them back.

Don't Use Humor

Darren LaCroix, the 2001 World Champion of Public Speaking and humorist, has extolled the value of humor in every presentation. He has implied — or rather "Darren-teed" — that your audience will laugh and have fun as they learn. I don't care what he says! If you want to lose your audience, ignore his advice!

If you insist on using humor, there are effective ways to do so. Never use self-depreciating humor. I don't care that David Brooks, the 1990 World Champion of Public Speaking, has advocated this type of humor! Why give the audience a reason to have fun at your expense? The key is to pick on someone in your audience and make fun of them! Find someone who's already vulnerable and uncomfortable just being at the event and make them the target of your jokes. Identify someone who doesn't expect or want attention and get the entire audience to laugh at them.

To maximize the impact, use bawdy, ribald, and distasteful humor at every opportunity. Better yet, use ethnic humor that is guaranteed to offend and embarrass everyone in the room. You'll lose your audience very quickly, and they won't exit laughing.

Don't Make a Point

This technique is the ultimate application of using the wisdom of Confuse-Us and meandering. Giving your audience a valuable message could keep them in their seats, or worse, motivate them to come back for more! When you give a call-to-action to conclude your speech, that's a red flag that you may have inadvertently made a point. Replace it with another off-topic statistic.

If you have difficulty with this, here's a simple solution: just focus on yourself. Talk about your trip to the event, the kind of day, week, or year you're having. Remember to let them know why you're so much better than they are and how you arrived at your high station in life. They'll walk away with nothing of value — but the important thing is, they'll walk away!

Don't Involve the Audience

Never establish a relationship with your audience. Never let them think that you have anything in common with them and never ever interact with them. I know I've been quoted as saying, "As much as the audience wants to hear you, they really want to know you!" but people who don't care about their audience reply, "Nonsense! Ignore that bald-headed Jamaican man! He has no idea what he's talking about."

In my experience, an audience that's involved and engaged often learns more and establishes a bond with the speaker. That's not what you want, so never give them an opportunity to participate in the program. If you want to lose your audience, make sure that they're totally detached from the process.

Remember, an audience that speaks up is an audience that shows up. You're the star — why would you let them do any of the work?

Don't Tell Stories

For years, we've heard 1990 World Champion of Public Speaking David Brooks refer to advice from Bill Gove: "Make a point, tell a story. Make another point, tell another story." Rubbish! Bill Gove is only the first president of the National Speakers Association. What does he know?

Almost as powerful are irrelevant statistics and pointless meandering in a rapid-fire, point-after-point-after-point delivery with no stories to relate the information to real life. Your audience will be brain-dead trying to absorb it all.

But What If the Speaker Just Loves to Tell Stories?

If you must tell a story, then make one up! Call it "narrative license," and it is yours to use as you see fit. If you aren't creative enough, then hijack someone else's story! Just plagiarize! Go to your local bookstore and buy a book of stories that you can steal. Better yet, don't even buy the book! Just find a few stories that you like, and jot them down for later reference. A few easy targets are the *Chicken Soup for the Soul* series and *Reader's Digest*.

If going to a bookstore is too much trouble, just fall back on an old staple: talk about yourself. It's important to always make yourself the hero of your story, so hyperbole is very important. If you walked a quarter mile, make it three miles — uphill in a blizzard! If you were startled by a Chihuahua, tell about a snarling pack of Rottweilers or Pit Bulls. The important thing is to make the story all about you.

Remember, it isn't about connecting with your audience by being truthful — it is about impressing them with your self-importance.

Don't Let Your Audience Think You Care

Don't be concerned about your audience. Just talk about what's important to you with no regard for what they may think or feel. If you really want to lose your audience, make no attempt to establish a connection with them, show empathy, or exhibit any sign that you care about them.

Always plow "full speed ahead" with YOUR agenda, YOUR purpose, and YOUR goal. The audience is there to validate you. Even if you're tempted to show signs of compassion — or worse, genuine interest in them and the issues they face — resist!

Remember the adult learning theory that says, "The answers are in the room." You don't want them to start solving their own problems, do you? What kind of a speaker would you be if you empowered your audience?

Final Thoughts

So that's it. If you want to get rid of pesky audiences, just follow these ten obnoxious rules and you'll lose your audience before you're done speaking every time!

World Champions' EDGE Testimonial

AWESOME! Finally a resource with excellent content, tools, and a networking platform that I can use when and where I am. I love the taped lessons, the ability for content review by peers, and most of all the opportunity to learn from such a wide variety of speakers and levels. Thanks you for creating such an exciting supportive venue!

Julia Bowlin MD, Versailles, Ohio

World Champions' EDGE Testimonial

"One of the powerful EDGE learning tools that has benefited me are the weekly audio lessons. I don't have a lot of free time, and the format of these short informative messages is excellent. They cover specific tips and techniques and give examples. I listen to them repeatedly, and they help take my speech development to a new level."

Rich Bassemir, Austin, Texas

CHAPTER 5
Speak into the Listening That People Are Hearing
The Five Ways People Listen and How to Connect Deeply with Them

by Ed Tate

Have you ever been struck by a profound statement — one that stopped you in your tracks? Or maybe you did not realize the depth of the statement until later.

Last year, while working on a project in the auto industry, I had such an experience. I was working with a long-time friend and colleague, Doug Krug. Doug is the cofounder of the consulting firm Enlightened Leadership Solutions. He is also the coauthor of the Simon & Shuster best seller, *Enlightened Leadership: Getting to the Heart of Change*. In addition, Doug is an amazing speaker. He has the ability to connect with audience members no matter how diverse — and he's able to do it every single time.

How many of you would like to be able to do that every time that you spoke? Would you like to know Doug's secret for connecting with audiences on a deeper level?

Doug's profound statement sounded awkward and odd: "We must speak into the listening that people are hearing."

My interpretation of what Doug meant is that we must be able to speak in such a way that people will hear us. Great speakers are great listeners. They are able to speak into the listening that their audiences are hearing.

According to Tim Ursiny, PhD, author of *The Coward's Guide to Conflict*, there are five ways that people listen:

- Appreciative
- Empathic
- Comprehensive
- Discerning
- Evaluative

Appreciative Listener

Appreciative listeners like to have fun and be entertained. In this listening mode, they want to relax and enjoy the listening experience. The symbol that represents them is a remote control because this type of listener loses interest easily and "switches channels."

- **Goal:** Enjoyment and fun
- **Attributes:** They want to be entertained. They enjoy good stories, jokes, concerts, or comedy clubs.
- **Symbol:** Remote control — they switch channels and lose interest easily
- **Ask:** How does my speech keep an appreciative listener interested? Is it fun?

Empathic Listener

Empathic listeners are listening in order to support the speaker. Their focus is concern for the person talking. Empathic listening is generally used when counseling a friend, letting someone blow off steam, or bonding to create a relationship.

- **Goal:** Show concern or support for the person talking
- **Attributes:** You will see them nodding in agreement to show support.
- **Symbol:** Heart
- **Ask:** How is my talk appealing to the empathic listener?

Comprehensive Listener

Comprehensive listeners organize information provided by the speaker. They want to make sense of the information so they can apply it in their world. The symbol for listeners in this mode is the label maker. Labels give them structure and make the information easier to organize.

- **Goal:** Organize information or thoughts
- **Attributes:** They need organization so they can apply what they learn.
- **Symbol:** Label maker — labels give them a structure which gives them comfort.
- **Ask:** How can a comprehensive listener follow my presentation? Is it organized? Is it easy to label?

Discerning Listener

A discerning listener looks for the big picture or the most important point. They gather and sort through a lot information and focus on the most important point. In this listening mode, the listener asks a lot of questions.

- **Goal:** Find big picture or critical point
- **Attributes:** They ask many questions.
- **Symbol:** Question mark
- **Ask:** In what ways does my speech answer the questions of the discerning listener? Can they see the big picture with the clues that I provide?

Evaluative Listener

The most common style of listening in business is the evaluative mode. These listeners are listening in order to take action or move on a decision. Their symbol is the wrench because they are attempting to fix something. This listener is skeptical so you need to ask, "What information will help make a decision or fix a problem?"

- **Goal:** Take action, make a decision, or fix a problem
- **Attributes:** Their purpose in listening is to make a decision.
- **Symbol:** Wrench
- **Ask:** What information will help make a decision or fix a problem? Is my information credible?

Final Thoughts

Depending on the purpose of your speech, you may not want to appeal to all five listening styles. However, the more styles you incorporate, the more likely you are to be speaking into the listening that your audience is hearing.

World Champions' EDGE Testimonial

"I have been member of the EDGE since its beginnings. I have used its benefits on numerous occasions from the outstanding advice, monthly EDGE calls, CDs, and speech evaluations to networking and staying in contact with other EDGE members. What I have learned is invaluable. My skill level as a presenter has grown and that is evidenced by the number workshops I now hold. The EDGE is like having your own personal coach, mentor, and partner. If you're serious about being a better presenter, then being on board with the EDGE is an outstanding choice."

Mike Gerrick, Warren, Ohio

World Champions' EDGE Testimonial

 *"I have benefited in many ways from being an EDGE member such as being on the monthly calls, listening to the educational CDs, and writing on the EDGE Forum. Probably the most important benefit was the connection that Darren helped me establish with Orphan Train's speaker Charlotte Endorf who also wrote several books about the subject.*

Charlotte invited me to speak at the 2008 Orphan Train's Celebration in Fremont, Nebraska. She also asked me to contribute my personal story about being an orphan from the Home for Little Wanderers in Boston, Massachusetts in her book **Unsung Neighbors!** *Now I will have a product to sell and plan on donating 10 percent of the proceeds to the Home for Little Wanderers — all thanks to being a Champions' EDGE member since 2007.*

Sherri Raftery MEd, Saugus, Massachusetts

CHAPTER 6
Eight Keys to an Effective Q & A Session

by Craig Valentine

A question and answer (Q & A) session is a great way to engage your audience members in your speech. It also helps you manage the flow of your presentation while answering their additional questions. Here are eight keys to leading an effective question and answer session.

Set Expectations

Tell the audience how many questions you will take or how long you will entertain questions. For example, I usually say, "We will take four or five questions, and then I will wrap up the message." Or I might say, "We have five minutes for questions and then, we will put a bow on the message for today."

Along with setting expectations, you should also let your audience know that this is not the end. I add, "… and then we will wrap up the message," because audiences are used to most speakers ending with the Q & A. Because they might think you are at the end, it could prompt them to start packing up their papers and shuffling around in anticipation of leaving. You can solve this by setting the right expectations at the beginning of the Q & A.

Ask "What Questions Do You Have?"

When you are kicking off the Q & A portion, do not ask, "Do you have any questions?" or "Are there any questions?" People might not respond to these questions. Instead, ask, "What questions do you have?" This is no longer about whether or not they have a question; it is about what questions they have and how many. Questions will flow easily if you prompt them in an open-ended way rather than using the yes-or-no question.

Rephrase the Questions

Rephrasing questions accomplishes the following three things:

- It affirms the person who asked the question and makes him or her feel understood.
- It helps the other audience members understand what was asked because many times the questioner does not have a microphone.
- It gives you time to formulate your response.

Frame Your Responses

Give people an idea of how your response will be structured. For example, if it is going to be a three-part response, let them know what to expect. You might say, "There are three critical strategies you can use. First … second … and finally …" This way, even if you do speak a little longer than you want, it will not feel like you are rambling. It will still be a structured response.

Make Sure Your Answers Are Brief

Anticipate what audience members will ask. Prepare for those answers in advance so they are concise and succinct. The longer you take to answer, the quicker they will stop believing you. When you ramble on and on, your audience members think, "He's trying to find an answer somewhere in there." To them, it feels like you are throwing answers against a wall to see what sticks. Avoid doing that. Instead, give them short and powerful bursts that are well-phrased with lines they can easily remember and repeat. If they cannot easily repeat what you said, then you spoke too much.

Include the Whole Audience

Try to call on questioners from all four major sections of your audience. Call on someone in the front, the back, to the left, and to the right. Make them all feel involved.

Acknowledge the Importance or Validity of the Question

I know some speakers say, "Do not tell people they asked a good question because then everyone else you did not say that to will get offended." Let them be offended. If somebody gets offended because you praised someone else, that is their personal problem, not yours. Occasionally saying "great question" does much more good than harm. However, only say it if you mean it.

Occasionally Ask, "Does that Make Sense?"

Do not overdo it, but do use it — especially if you are not sure you addressed the person's question adequately or you read uncertainty on the person's face (or heard it in the person's voice). It does not hurt to check.

Final Thoughts

If you incorporate these eight keys into your question-and-answer period, you will keep deepening your connection with each response without destroying the flow of your speech.

World Champions' EDGE Testimonial

 *"It has been such an opportunity to meet and learn from some of the best speakers in the world. I look forward to listening to the weekly audio lessons, and because they are brief and to the point, you get great tips that are simple and easy to implement.*

The networking with fellow EDGE members has been amazing too. I have met some truly remarkable and like-minded people. The feedback, support, commentary, and camaraderie on the forums are fantastic! It was also great to meet Darren, Craig, David, Ed, and Mark and to meet several EDGE members face to face that I had met via the website.

The discount offers to members and the affiliate program are pretty cool as well. Where else do you get to hang out with four World Champs and one of the top professional speaking coaches in the world? For the price of a couple of pizzas per month, it provides such value for money!"

Craig Strachan, Cape Town, South Africa

CHAPTER 7

A Powerful Presentation Lesson From Dr. Wayne Dyer

by Darren LaCroix

As a presenter, have you ever walked into a packed room with lots of energy and couldn't wait for your chance to take the stage? It is exciting! On the flip side, have you ever walked into a room with only 25 percent of the seats filled and no energy? How do you feel? Does it affect your presentation? It used to hurt mine terribly.

Dr. Wayne Dyer is a very spiritually based motivational author and speaker. Some of his favorite quotes are: "You'll see it when you believe it," and "Stay focused on what you are for rather than what you are against." When I was first introduced to the world of motivation, I loved listening to Zig Ziglar, Tony Robbins, Brian Tracy, and Dr. Dyer.

I was at a church one day watching his film, *Ambition to Meaning*. One of my favorite quotes from that movie is "What we believe in the morning of our life, in the evening is a lie." It took me a while to understand what he meant by that. As we grow in life (or as a presenter), we must realize that some of the things we believed and lived by are not true anymore. We must let go. As fellow World Champion of Public Speaking Craig Valentine would say, "What got you here, won't get you there."

As I watched the film, I remembered a lesson I learned from him at one of his live presentations — a lesson I still need to be reminded of on occasion.

Dr. Dyer came to Worcester, Massachusetts early in my career. I had read his book, *Real Magic,* and could not wait to see him live. I was a new speaker at the time, and as I entered the room, I was getting excited. This is what I wanted to do for a living, and here was a celebrity in the business. Cool!

The room was set for a thousand people. One of the local insurance companies had brought him in to speak to their company and decided to open it up to the public to help cover the cost of bringing him in.

Seven minutes before show time, I looked around and saw that only about 25 percent of the seats were filled. Oh my! What a difficult setting. How uncomfortable for the speaker. I was embarrassed that there were so few people there. It was weird; I felt bad for him but I had nothing to do with the promotion of the event.

As Dr. Dyer took the stage, he had a certain calmness about him. He carefully looked around and noticed the light turnout. Someone must have said something to him or apologized to him for the low turnout. The first thing he said to the audience was, "It is okay. The people who are supposed to be here are. That's all we need." Wow! It took me awhile to absorb the impact of what he said.

At that point in my career, I would have freaked out. I would have been upset with someone. Bottom line: to him, it did not matter. He was okay with it. He did not let it affect him. In fact, he was excited to help whoever was there even though the setting was not perfect. We all need to remember that, yes, we want to have a full room with lots of energy. However, sometimes it won't be.

Once we optimize the setting for our presentation, our goal as a speaker is to help the people in front of us the best we can, no matter what the setting, or how many people are there. As much fun as a full room can be, we are there to change the lives and inspire the ones who are present. Don't let your own ego get in the way of your connection with your audience like I used to.

Final Thoughts

Dr. Dyer, thanks for helping me to "grow up" as a speaker. Thanks for helping me to see that confidence on stage is good, ego is not. How will you look at the next presentation when there is a low turnout?

Content Excellence

CHAPTER 8

Ignite Your Audience with Your Introduction

Point Your Speech in the Right Direction Before You Even Start Talking

by Craig Valentine

Please read the following paragraph aloud as if you're using it to introduce the next speaker with this typical introduction:

> "Our next speaker is the 1999 World Champion of Public Speaking. With more than 175,000 Toastmasters in 68 countries and over 25,000 contestants, he came home with the first prize trophy and a significant amount of national and international recognition.
>
> In addition, our speaker is absolutely oblivious to the fact that we could care less what he has done and that we are much more interested in what we will be able to do after hearing him. Moreover, our speaker seems to have no idea that we are simply hoping for his autobiographical introduction to end so we can start clapping as if we are interested. Finally, he doesn't realize that we are beginning to say to ourselves, 'His entire introduction is about him; therefore, I'll bet his entire speech is about him also. Why did I even come here today?'
>
> So, with that said, please help me welcome to the stage — the person who would have the least-effective introduction in history if it weren't for the thousands of other presenters who have introductions just like his — the 1999 World Champion of Public Speaking, Craig Valentine."

What's Wrong with That Introduction?

Do you get the point? How similar is your introduction to the one that you read above?

Is it about YOU or is it about what YOUR AUDIENCE will get out of your speech? Everything you do should be about the audience — including your introduction.

Your introduction flavors your entire speech. You can use it to get the audience fired up and excited about what they're going to hear, or you can use it to boost yourself up in their eyes. You can use it to whet their appetite with the valuable tools they are sure to get from your presentation, or, again, you can use it to boost yourself up in their eyes. Here's one thing I know for sure; once I changed my introduction from "me-focused" to "you-focused," I gave myself an extreme advantage before I even said one word.

Five Guideposts to Fire Up Your Audience with Your Introduction

An effective introduction is the difference between starting off in a hole or on solid ground. Here are some nuts-and-bolts tools you can use in your introduction to get off to a great start with your very next speech. Don't go into your next speech without them.

Start It Off about Them

Make your very first sentence about them. Instead of starting with "Our next speaker today is the 1999 World Champion ..." start with something like the following:

> "There is a definite process for keeping your audiences on the edge of their seats. It is not easy to come by, and it is not easy to use. However, once you master it, you WILL find doors opening for you that you never even knew existed."

You might have noticed there were five "you" words used in those two sentences. Make it you-focused first. Start with them; not with yourself. How many you-related words are in your introduction? Count them and make sure there are many more you-related words than there are I-related words.

Make a Promise

Let them know not only what they will get, but also what those tools will empower them to do and to receive. In the example above, I tell them they will get a process that empowers them to keep their audiences on the edge of their seats and rewards them with more open doors and opportunities. That's a pretty compelling promise. What compelling promise do you make with your introduction?

Build Your Credibility But Only with Your Relevant Credentials

I have a specific introduction for my team-building workshops. This specific introduction includes a piece that mentions how I won three consecutive East Coast Conference Championships and played in two NCAA March Madness tournaments as a college basketball player. Because this part of my history relates to teams, it belongs in this introduction on team building. However, as proud as I am about those basketball accomplishments, do you think they belong in my introduction if the speech is about presentation skills? If I was sitting in the audience and I heard them say, "Our presentation coach today was also a college basketball player," I know I'd be thinking, "Well, while he was dribbling up and down the court, was he giving speeches? If not, why do I care about his basketball past?" Only use the relevant information no matter how well-rounded you are. Even if you are extremely proud of something, don't force something to fit. Instead, leave it out. Is all the information in your introduction relevant to the subject at hand?

Use the Introduction to Set Up Something in Your Speech

When I begin speaking, I often call back to my introduction by saying the following:

> "Do you know, that even with all those accolades, people still don't like me? Do you know why they don't like me?"

Then I go into a humorous story about why they don't like me, but it all is set up by the accolades (relevant ones) in my introduction. Find ways to make your introduction seamlessly feed into your speech. How do you currently tie your speech back into your introduction?

Take Everything about You and Turn It into Everything for Them

If you do this, your audience will be ready and excited to receive your message. For example, instead of stating, "Craig Valentine is the 1999 World Champion of Public Speaking," I could make that actually matter to them by saying:

> "The process you will pick up today helped our speaker become the 1999 World Champion, and you can use it to become a speaker in high demand."

Final Thoughts

Turn everything about you into something for them. Doing this will get them fired up to hear your message. It tickles me now because when the introducer gets to the end of my introduction, he or she usually says, "Are you ready for the process?" At this point, people actually begin yelling out, "Yes!" That is some great energy to walk into for a speech.

Follow the five guideposts listed here and watch as your audience leans forward in their seats and anxiously awaits your presentation. That's how you ignite your audience with your introduction.

World Champions' EDGE Testimonial

"I auditioned in New York City for a contract with a national seminar company and won. There were twenty-one other speakers. Each of us had to deliver a ten-minute presentation. My content, delivery style, use of stories, economy of words, arriving ninety minutes early, and establishing a rapport with the recruiter were all influenced by my EDGE association. If you absorb as much as possible and apply what you learn as an EDGE member, it will fast-track your success as a speaker."

John Aviste, Black River, New York

World Champions' EDGE Testimonial

"There are so many reasons to join the EDGE. I have to pick just one? Okay, just one reason, in just one word — specificity. In the EDGE, you don't just get vague generalities or opinions. You get specific ideas to improve and real-world examples of how those ideas HAVE worked for Darren, Ed, Mark, Craig, or Fripp.

But wait! There's more! Every month, you have the opportunity to ask the EDGE faculty your own questions **specific** *to your own situation or your own speeches. So if you have a question, as I did, on how to approach someone for an interview, you can ask and get a specific, real-world answer.*

One more specific reason to join the EDGE — e-critiques. As an EDGE member, you get the opportunity to submit a speech to any of the Champs and get advice on how to improve it. You can't get more specific than that. For example, here is what I wrote to David Brooks after my first e-critique back in April of 2006:

'Wow ... so this is coaching. Why didn't I start earlier? Your comments and suggestions for my speech were insightful, powerful, and enlightening. By suggesting two sentences, you took something that I merely implied in my original speech, made that explicit, then answered a question that I had made merely rhetorical ... and so drove the point home.

I am stunned by your review of my speech. The quality of your evaluation alone is worth this month's Champions' EDGE investment ... and the next six as well. I am busy writing the transitions you suggested I write and incorporating your other suggestions to improve my speech. I can't wait to learn even more in this program.'

Join the EDGE and get real-world, specific advice to improve your speaking."

Michael Erwine, Eaton Rapids, Michigan

CHAPTER 9
Mind Your Ps and Qs
A Presenter's Perspective on an Old-Fashioned Nugget of Advice

by Mark Brown

As a child growing up in Jamaica, I was often admonished by my parents when visiting someone's house or going away from home to "mind my Ps and Qs." It was a reminder to be on my best behavior. Whenever you deliver a presentation, minding your Ps and Qs helps make a deep and respectful connection with others. Since that's exactly what we want to do with an audience, let's look at some Ps and Qs for preparing and presenting speeches.

Poetry and Quotations

Poetry and quotations are effective tools for capturing an audience's attention. You can use them to connect with your audience through that which is familiar — and conversely, to attract their attention by using something which is obscure in their minds.

Think about it: have you ever heard a speaker use a familiar bit of poetry early in their speech? You can tell by the audience's reaction that they're well-acquainted with the material and can relate to it. It's a powerful way to reinforce a point.

Similarly, quotations are wonderful tools. A well-chosen quotation can serve as an effective speech opener or a strong anchor in the middle of a presentation. I have also seen quotations, poetry, and well-known prose used at the end of a speech to reinforce the points that were covered.

Let me emphatically add that when using poetry and quotations, the idea is to reinforce your point, not to overtake it. I've seen speech contestants use two, three, or even four quotations in their seven-minute speeches. One contestant used a quotation that lasted thirty seconds. While it was an effective use of a quotation, I would have liked to see the speaker use more original material. The audience wants to hear from you. They want originality — your thoughts, your ideas, your perspective, your take on the world.

If you're involved in a speech contest, your judges are looking for original thought and how you present your ideas, concepts, and worldview. Poetry and quotations are effective tools, but you should use them judiciously.

In my presentation at the Toastmasters International 1995 World Championship of Public Speaking, I opened with the quotation, "You never get a second chance to make a first impression." It lasted only four seconds, but it was effective.

Use relevant poetry when you recognize an appropriate moment. Use quotations when they support your message. Just don't let them overtake your message, outweighing everything else in your speech. They are simply tools to support and reinforce your point.

Preponderance and Quantity

As you continue to prepare yourself to deliver a great presentation, you need to be mindful of the preponderance (the weight and heaviness of your content) and quantity of your material.

This P-and-Q combo refers to the amount of material that we give to the audience at one time. Sometimes we try to give the audience everything that we have to offer — and in the process, we present much more than they can handle . We give them a "sensory overload." We want to tell our best stories, but sometimes we tell too many stories.

As I was preparing my speech for the 1995 World Championship of Public Speaking, I was determined to tell three stories to drive my point home. Why? I was taught about "the power of three." At the time, I had two very good stories but I just had to find a third. As I began to struggle, fight, and agonize over this, I finally asked myself, "Why do you need a third story? Where is it written in granite that without a third story, the speech will fail?" It was then that I realized that I didn't need a third story. So I prepared my speech with the two good stories that I had, and I used them very effectively.

During a speech coaching session at a World Champion Speakers Champ Camp, one of the participants delivered a good speech, but she had enough material to present TWO speeches. If you are a Toastmaster, the average length of your speech may be six or seven minutes. However, if you try to cram four or five stories into a seven-minute speech, you may give the audience too much to process at one time.

Bill Gove is credited with the quotation, "Make a point, tell a story. Make another point, tell another story." The operative words in the quotation are "a" and "another." Sometimes in our eagerness to illustrate a point, we are tempted to tell two or three stories even when the point has already been made, and the story has already been effective. If you make three points and support each point with three stories, you will have told the audience nine stories just to make three points. That's just too much.

True, your audience may be sophisticated enough to glean your points amidst so many stories, but why overwhelm them? By spending so much time telling stories, you deprive the audience of the opportunity to learn more. Time used telling more stories could be better spent sharing more information. As you prepare your presentation, give thought to how many points you wish to make and how many stories you will tell.

Poetry, quotations, preponderance, and quantity are key components in the preparation process. What follows are very familiar Ps and Qs that affect our presentation.

Pace and Quickness

Pace and quickness have a dramatic impact on delivery. My appreciation for appropriate pace and quickness of delivery came in 2001 when I was invited to speak in the Kingdom of Bahrain. I had to come to terms with the fact that I was a Jamaican living in the United States of America who was addressing an Asian audience whose primary language was not my own (English). It was clear that to be respectful — and more importantly to be understood — I had to be mindful of the pace and quickness of my delivery.

You show respect for your audience when you speak slowly and clearly, especially if you have a distinct accent as I do. You should give them time to fully comprehend and process what you have said. The audience is the priority — it's not about us. While your desire to drive your point home is great, it is more important to insure that the pace and quickness of your delivery does not make your audience uncomfortable. It should be able to receive all that you have to offer.

Pause and Quietness

To support this goal, another P-and-Q combination is important: pause and quietness. Don't confuse them. The former concern was speaking rate, whereas the latter concern relates to the time spent allowing the audience to process what they are hearing. Some speakers fail to utilize the pause and quietness effect, and this failure sometimes stems from the first P-and-Q combination mentioned: preponderance and quantity.

We must give the audience time to experience emotions, to digest what we have said, and to decide how they will respond to our words. The pauses can be very effective, and the quiet moments offer the opportunity for reflection. My favorite example of the effective use of quietness came from my good friend, the 1999 World Champion of Public Speaking, Craig Valentine, as he delivered his winning speech during that competition.

Craig spoke about the importance of spending five minutes of each day in silence. To drive his point home, he ended his speech in SILENCE! As the well-known adage says, "The silence was deafening." Craig achieved his objective by using quietness masterfully. Craig understood the power of the pause and the quality of quietness. It was memorable. Pause and quietness, when used properly, will have an unforgettable effect on your audience.

Power and Quality

Poetry and quotations, preponderance and quantity, pace and quickness, pause and quietness — these are vital for effective platform presentation. When applied properly, they provide one more P-and-Q combination: power and quality.

This should be our ultimate goal: to deliver messages that are powerful and memorable. If the objective is humor, make the audience laugh. If it is informational, provide the audience with material that is useful and practical. It is not enough to impress our audiences with an excellent turn of phrase, dynamic platform skills, or charm and charisma. We must commit ourselves to delivering presentations of the highest quality every time we take the platform.

Final Thoughts

As you strive to leave your audience with a memorable experience, touch their heads, their hearts, and their hands by minding your Ps and Qs. These five combinations will help you deliver a powerful presentation.

World Champions' EDGE Testimonial

"I have been a member of the EDGE for almost two years and have found it to be an amazing resource. Every day, I am surprised at the new insights I get into my speaking from the Champs, Patricia Fripp, and my fellow EDGE members. It doesn't matter if you are a new speaker or a seasoned professional, the EDGE is the premier educational resource for speakers of all experience levels. If you are looking to learn how to better connect with the audience, how to develop amazing speeches, and how to go from 'chump to champ,' then you need to be on the EDGE. You won't regret it!"

Chris Elliott, Columbus, Ohio

CHAPTER 10
Speak to Be Remembered and Repeated

by Patricia Fripp

Speak to be remembered and repeated. Isn't that the goal of every communicator — to be remembered and repeated? This is a key idea I reinforce at every Fripp Speaking School. Actually, it is a key idea every time I have the opportunity to discuss speaking and presentation skills. Yes, it's easier said than done. Here are a few key ideas.

Speak in Shorter Sentences

Edit your sentences to a nub. Remember, comedian and television actor Jerry Seinfeld said, "I will spend an hour taking an eight-word sentence and making it five." In comedy, the fewer the words between the setup and the punch word, the bigger the laugh.

Choose the Best Punch Word

Here is an example. In the sentence, "You have to make an important decision today," your punch word should be "decision." So switch it around: "Today, you have to make an important DECISION!"

If you have a sentence with two important words or phrases, put the more important word at the end. "Today, YOU have to make an important DECISION." Or, "The important DECISION today is going to be made by YOU." Just be careful not to step on your punch word (it should be the final word or idea in the sentence).

Perfect Your Pause

Deliver your punch word and then pause — and pause — and pause. Give your listeners time to digest what you've just said. Get comfortable with silence, and don't be tempted to fill it with "ums."

Repeat Your Key Ideas More Than Once

Use repetition to drive your point home, create a reminder of a key point you want your audience to remember, add a dash of humor, or just to create a thread of continuity throughout your message.

Say Something Memorable

Let us look at a few recent examples from the memorial for *60 Minutes'* Ed Bradley. Fellow *60 Minutes* reporter Steve Kroft said, "I learned a lot from Ed Bradley, and not just about journalism. I learned a lot about friendship, manners, clothes, wine, freshly cut flowers — which he had delivered to his office every week — and the importance of stopping and smelling them every once in awhile."

Surprise guest Bill Clinton said, "Ed Bradley was a brilliant, insatiable, curious traveler on a relentless quest to get to the bottom of things. He was like the great jazz musicians he so admired. He always played in the key of reason. His songs were full of the notes of facts; but he knew to make the most of music, you have to improvise. We'll never forget what his solos were: the disarming smile; the disconcerting stare; the highly uncomfortable stretches of silence; the deceptively dangerous questions; and the questions that would be revealing, no matter what your answer."

Want Your Audiences to Remember What You Say? Learn the Importance of Clear Structure

When speaking in public, your message — no matter how important — will not be effective or memorable if you don't have a clear structure.

Can you write the premise or objective of your talk in one sentence? If not, the chances are good that your thinking isn't clear enough for the audience to understand your purpose. And if you don't organize your material so the audience can remember it easily, they'll have a hard time grasping your message. They may be dazzled by your pizzazz and laugh at your stories, but little will stay with them afterwards.

Your next structural imperative is to use statements that make your audience ask "How?" or "Why?" For example, during a talk on "Selling Yourself and Your Ideas to Upper Management," I say, "Everyone in your position can sell themselves and their ideas to upper management." Immediately, my audience is asking themselves, "HOW can I do that?" Or at another speech, I might say, "Every manager needs to develop employees who can think entrepreneurially." And the managers are all asking themselves, "WHY on earth do I need to do that?"

Your answers to their mental questions — their "hows" or "whys" — become your "points of wisdom" (the rationale for your premise or objective). Illustrate each point with stories, examples, suggestions, practical advice, or recommendations. Allow about ten minutes for each point of wisdom — an average of three in a thirty-minute presentation.

Finally, frame your premise and your points of wisdom with an attention-getting opening and a memorable closing. For example, I helped a neighbor who is a scientist named Mike Powell with a speech he was delivering to a general audience. I suggested that since most of us don't know what it is like to be a scientist, he should tell the audience. Mike captured everyone's attention by saying, "Being a scientist is like doing a jigsaw puzzle ... in a snowstorm ... at night ... when you don't have all the pieces ... and you don't have the picture you are trying to create."

Your last thirty seconds must send people out energized and fulfilled. Ask for questions before you close so you don't diffuse the effect of your ending. Then finish with something inspirational that supports your theme and creates a "circle" with your opening. My scientist friend Mike closed by saying, "At the beginning of my talk, I told you of the frustration of being a scientist. Many people ask, 'So why do you do it?'" Then Mike told them about the final speaker at a medical conference he attended. She walked to the lectern and said, "I am a thirty-two-year-old wife and mother of two. I have AIDS. Please work fast." Mike received a standing ovation for his speech. Even more important, several years later, the audience still remembers what he said and can actually quote him!

Five Tips for Exciting Speeches

Are you worried that your speeches lack pizzazz? Whether you are writing the speech for you or someone else to give, here are five tips to put some excitement in your message and your audience.

Open Hot, Close Hotter

To grab audience attention and be remembered, start the presentation with a bang, not a limp thanks-it's-nice-to-be-here opening. The first (and last) thirty seconds have the most impact on the audience. Save any greetings and gratitude until you've already grabbed the audience with a powerful opening.

And don't end with a whimper. Remember that last words linger. Unfortunately, many speakers close with, "Are there any questions?" Wrong! Instead, say, "Before I close, are there any questions?" Answer them. Then close on a high note.

Get the Inside Scoop

Attendees at one of my *How to Be a Coach to Your Client* seminars wanted to know how to personalize and add excitement and color to the speeches they craft for others. How, they ask, can they get those invaluable inside stories? I suggested they do what I do — interview the speaker's clients, colleagues, and family members. These people are familiar with the stories the speaker often tells — stories that have already been honed to what I call the "Hollywood model" (characters, dialogue, dramatic lesson learned). What insights and amusing stories can they share? Advise your members to ask others for input that can provide color and energy to a presentation.

Try Inside-Out Speaking

Don't write speeches for people to read. If you are writing a speech for someone else, sit down with them, in person or on the phone, and ask them questions. By doing this, you can pull out their ideas, stories, life experiences, philosophies, and examples through questions. When I'm writing a speech for a client and we've completed the interview, my job is to help them organize, wordsmith, and deliver these comments with more drama. Although the client and I often end up with a script that can then be edited and tightened, the words grow out of our conversations. I call this "inside-out" speaking. My work represents a cleaned-up conversation — one the speaker is going to have with the audience. Of course, a script is not a conversation, but if it sounds conversational, it is more appealing and much easier to deliver directly to the audience without reading it word for word.

Provide Five Magic Moments

How are great speeches like classic Hollywood movies? Movie promoters say that a successful film has to have five magic moments for each viewer, though not necessarily the same five for all viewers. When it does, people will talk about it and add enough energy to a paid advertising campaign to make it a hit. Be sure your presentation has five great moments — dramatic, humorous, profound, or poignant — that the audience can relive in their minds later and repeat to their friends.

Avoid Borrowed Stories

I urge you to create vivid, personal stories for your presentations. Imagine how I once felt — sitting in an audience of 18,000 people — listening to Barbara Bush describe a great story she had read in *Chicken Soup for the Soul* — my own story which made the point, "What you do speaks louder than what you say." (Yes, I know Ralph Waldo Emerson said it first.) Did Barbara Bush mention it was my story? No. But even if she had mentioned my name, I think she missed a huge opportunity with her speech.

Back then, I imagined her sitting in bed at the White House, going through stacks of books with a highlighter pen for things to talk about. Since then, I've realized that a speech writer did the research and wrote her words. My point? I'm not upset she didn't credit me. I'm just disappointed that someone with Barbara Bush's incredible life experiences did not share them. I am sure she had much more interesting recent topics and perceptions than reporting on something someone said to me many years ago. That's how audiences will feel if you repeat things you've read instead of experienced.

So You Want to Speak and Can't Think of What to Say

Effective communication and award-winning presentations must contain great content. Public speaking classes are full of tips on how to hold your hand, stand, and make eye contact. Important as all these habits and techniques are, you have to start with good original content.

Let's look at how you develop your original content. In my presentation skills training for professional speakers and business speaking training and coaching with executives, I am frequently asked, "What on earth do I speak about? Where do I find good examples?"

Explore Your Experiences

Here is my advice if your goal is to have effective business presentations. This advice applies whether you are in person in front of your audience or deliver your message as a webinar. The secret of developing good content is simply this: you have to live an interesting life and converse with interesting people.

Follow this process for analyzing and organizing your experiences.

1. Make a list of all the people who have influenced you in your life. Lists are a great way to trigger your memory of what you could talk about.

2. Make a list of every manager and boss you've ever worked for.

3. Write down what you learned from them. Even if they were a bad boss, they can serve at least as a pitiful example. Here's an example:

> When I was a fifteen-year-old shampoo girl, my first boss was Mr. Paul. I saw him treat every woman who came into our salon, for the time she was there, like she was the only one in the world. He treated the woman who worked as a waitress at the Carlton Hotel as well as the rich little lady who lived in the penthouse at the Carlton Hotel.
>
> When I was young, I thought that was good service. It was nice to treat people well. Now that I'm older, sophisticated, and in business, I reflect back and realize lessons learned that I wasn't sophisticated enough to understand.
>
> Now that I'm in business, promoting myself, and teaching other people, I realize that the waitress in the Carlton Hotel who talks to a somewhat affluent clientele of 150 to 200 people a day, has a sphere of influence a lot greater than the rich little lady who plays bridge every day with the same half dozen friends.

That's a lesson. I guarantee your lists will provide lessons learned. As you look at who influenced you and who your bosses were, ask yourself what they taught you and then how that plays out in your life now.

You might also want to remember and record all the turning points: the different jobs, schools, colleges, and seminars; who you met; when you fell in love with an idea, a profession, or a cause, etc. Look at the best advice that you've been given.

Conduct Good Market Research

As a hairstylist, I spent twenty-four years behind a hairstyling chair. When I was fifteen, we had many rich, glamorous women as customers. As soon as I got to know them, I used to say, "What were you doing when you were my age? How did you make your money? Did you make it yourself or did you marry it? If you made it yourself, how did you do it? If you married it, where did you meet him?"

My brother, internationally acclaimed guitarist Robert Fripp, is always saying, "Sister, you ask people such personal questions!" During my overlapping careers with twenty-four years behind a hairstyling chair and twenty-five years of going to conferences and speaking and asking questions, nobody has ever said, "That's none of your damn business." People love talking about themselves and asking questions is a great way to develop material.

Craft Your Information into a Story

Think about the advice. Think about the lessons learned. The best way to pull out these milestones is to sit down with a friend or a group of your pals who are also interested in developing their public speaking skills and do what I call the "Once upon a time ..." technique.

Tell a fairy tale of your life as if it was about someone else, and don't go into too much detail. Here is an example.

> "Once upon a time there was a little girl born in England. She had a brother who was one year, one month, two days, twelve-and-a-half hours younger than she was. He was always a very smart kid — top of the class. She worked hard and was about fifteenth in a class of thirty. Her dad sold houses for a living and became a very successful businessperson.
>
> When she was twelve, she decided she was probably more artistic than academic, so she decided to become a hairstylist. When she was fifteen, she left school and served a three-year apprenticeship and really learned about customer service — as well as hairstyling — from her boss.

When she used to go to work on the bus, all her little friends were talking about marrying millionaires, but at fifteen, she realized it's much better to become a millionaire than to marry one.

When she was eighteen, she left home and went to live on an island off France called Jersey. She worked with sophisticated gentlemen from the west end of London who could do hairstyles she'd never seen before.

However, she thought lunch hours were for squeezing in three extra customers, whereas the other guys thought that lunch hours were for eating lunch. One day her boss told her she actually produced thirty percent more income for the salon, not by being better, but by working much harder. She realized that perhaps tenacity and the willingness to work hard were more valuable than great talent. But where to promote it — obviously the colonies."

I've just gone through my life as if I was talking about someone else, almost as if it were a fairy tale. Go through your time line using the "Once upon a time ..." technique. Then get your friends to ask you the questions that are stimulated from your time line. Note the high points, what your friends are interested in hearing about, what people ask you about at a cocktail party when they know what you do for a living, and what your interests are. These are the type of things that an audience would want to know.

Your lists and life time line can help you develop content and material for your presentations. Every single day, carry around a notepad and reflect at the end of the day. Ask yourself, "What happened to me today that could one day be used in a speech?" If you had good customer service or bad customer service, it's still a story and an example. Search your life for the stories that have a message. Now use what you've learned to develop good, original content.

Four Strong Openings

I have so frequently heard some of the Toastmasters World Champions of Public Speaking say, "You have to open strong." The first thirty seconds and the last thirty seconds of most presentations are going to be strong and memorable. If you want to be invited back, if you want people to talk about what you're saying, make sure you come out punching. Let's look at four good ways to open a presentation.

An Original or Interesting Story — *[handwritten: something to do w/ your life]* *[handwritten: for a sales presentation]*

If this is a sales presentation, perhaps it would be a story of a satisfied client. When I say original, I mean a story that has something to do with your life or your experience. It shouldn't be a story that somebody could read in *Chicken Soup for the Soul*, nor is it a classic cliché story such as "the starfish story." If you don't know what I mean by "the starfish story," it has been told for years by the late Og Mandino, Zig Ziglar, and dozens of other would-be motivational speakers.

A Powerful Quotation

Even though there's so much truth in the world, the audience is benefiting from your wisdom. When you're looking at a powerful quotation, it doesn't have to be by Abraham Lincoln, John F. Kennedy, or Benjamin Franklin. It could be something your grandmother, your first boss, or your best client said. It could be something that you know the audience would never have heard before and find interesting and valuable.

You have thirty seconds to command the attention of your audience. Don't waste it! General Eisenhower said, "Leadership is the ability to decide what has to be done and then to get people to want to do it." When I talk on leadership, I might start with that quote. I'm also a believer in quoting other people besides "dead white men" — not that many haven't said wonderful things.

Instead, consider quoting live individuals. When I'm talking about getting and keeping customers, I say, "As Bill Gates said, 'When you lose a customer, you lose two ways. First, you don't get their money. And second, your competitor does.'" I also add a pantomime by stabbing myself in the heart, which usually gets a laugh.

Quotes can be both informative and surprising. As actress Raquel Welch philosophically noted, "Style is being yourself, but on purpose." I add, "Every time you stand up to address an audience, you have to be yourself, but slightly larger than life, in other words — on purpose."

It seems to me, too many speakers use sports stars or often over-quoted sources that the audience is very familiar with. Be creative. If your audience has not heard your quotes before, your entire message will seem fresher and more original. A great source of quotes is the audience you are addressing or those they know. At a four-day Texas Instruments (TI)

Opening Options

Based on getting paid to speak for more than twenty-five years and coaching other speakers, executives, and sales teams, I am amazed how few people know how to start their presentation. Here are a list of techniques and actual phrases that I have used or coached others to use. Hope it helps you!

The Techniques

- Story
- A little-known fact
- Interesting statistic
- Powerful quotation
- Rhetorical question
- Relate to the situation, introduction, or introducer
- A challenge
- Startling statement
- Relate to a corporate report, program, or headlines
- Tie into the meeting theme
- Bold claim or promise
- Find immediate connection to the audience (So what? Me too!)
- Recommendation first (business presentations)
- Significance of your topic
- A needed explanation
- Mention what is on the mind of the audience
- Read a letter or review
- Transport them to a different place or time "Imagine …"
- Dictionary definition of words in the theme
- Compliment the audience
- Relevant joke (not recommended unless original)
- Refer to something earlier in the program
- Remember a special date or cause
- Poem or song

Patricia Fripp's Theatrical Choices within the Structure
- Once upon a time
- Begin with the end in mind
- In medius res
- Past, present, or future
- Five questions

The Words
- I wish you could have been there …
- I'll never forget the first time …
- It was one of the most exciting days of my life …
- It was the scariest moment of my life …
- It was not exactly what I expected …
- What would the world be like without …
- I love your theme …
- If I were to ask you …
- Who would have thought …
- Remember the good old days when …
- It was just one of those days …
- I will never forget the time when …
- There I was, my very first day …
- You have an awesome responsibility …
- Just like you, I was brought up to believe …
- Come back with me …
- Imagine …
- Let's start with a history lesson …
- The year was …
- Suddenly, everything fell into place …
- As I was growing up, my dad always said …
- You know what it is like when …
- Have you ever had the feeling that …
- To put this report into historical perspective …

conference, I told the audience, "I'm here to tell you how to future-proof your careers." I had heard their chairman use the phrase "future-proof" two days earlier. He said the TI strategy was to future-proof the shareholders' investment. I borrowed his words to connect with the audience, though they were actually technology users, not investors. The phrase already had the company stamp of approval.

Good quotes can be sprinkled throughout your talk. What made that engagement so successful was the fact I quoted every single person who had spoken on the program before me over the prior three days.

Any important or recent quote related to the industry or organization you are addressing can get you immediate attention and establish a connection between you and your listeners. I often quote something from my client's most recent corporate report. Clients tell me, "We're so glad you quoted our chairman. We always send the report to our associates, but we don't think they ever read it."

Make a List of Original Sources

Do you have any quotes from:

- Your father, mother, siblings, grandmother/father
- A teacher or coach
- Your first boss or managers who inspired you
- Your brilliant or successful clients
- Yourself!

Here are some of my favorite quotes (use if you want; just give me credit):

- **My Father, A.H. Fripp:** "Don't concentrate on making a lot of money, but rather concentrate on becoming the type of person people want to do business with, and you most likely will make a lot of money."
- **My Mother, Edie Fripp:** "Of course it is the inner you that counts, but dress up and look good so you can attract people so they can find out how nice you are, how smart you are, and how valuable you can be to them."
- **My Brother, Robert Fripp:** "Discipline is not an end in itself, but a means to an end."
- **My Brilliant Hairstyling Client, Manny Lozano** (from my days as a men's hairstylist for fifteen years): "Keep promoting even when your

appointment calendar is full. You need to resell the clients you have that this is still the place they want to come."

- **Patricia Fripp:** "The only thing I ever wanted in business is an unfair advantage."

Here is note of caution however: make sure you chose a quote that is not overused. Even if you have a great quote that really makes the point of your speech, carefully consider not using it if everyone in the audience could finish the sentence for you. For example, "We have nothing to fear but fear itself" or "Ask not ..." — the great Kennedy line — is perhaps too overexposed. I'm not saying don't use it in the presentation. I just wouldn't start the presentation with it. The opening sets the flavor of the presentation. You always want your opening to be fresh and interesting, or the audience will be thinking, "Oh, there's nothing new I haven't heard."

A Thought-Provoking Question

When I suggest that you use a question, I don't mean that you should ask, "Will you raise your hand if you want to make more money?" If you ask a question that requires an answer and the audience does not respond the way you hope and expect, that's when the perspiration starts running down your back, and you beg feel nervous. Not every audience is responsive or even happy to be there. Many of our audiences are forced to go to be "fixed" by the speaker their organization hired, or perhaps they are tired and exhausted by the time you speak.

Therefore, I recommend you ask a question rhetorically. You could use these words: "If I were to ask you, 'Is this the year you make more money,' perhaps you would say, 'Patricia, I make enough. I don't care,' or 'Patricia, I'd like to; show me how.'" You see, in this example, what we are doing is posing the question and giving a list of what the answers might be.

An Interesting Statistic or Little-Known Fact

Here is one of my favorite examples. I was in an audience and speaking for the Young Presidents organization. One of the other speakers was Newt Gingrich. He walked out and said, "If you were born today, you would already owe $186,000 to pay off your share of the national debt."

That fact was good for two reasons — well actually three if you consider he just came out and opened the speech with that fact. It was an interesting statistic that we didn't know, and even if you don't like him politically, you would want to know what comes next.

He also gets a double-whammo point from me because there were three "yous" and not a single "I." That makes it an audience-advocate opening or high "I:You Ratio" as I call it.

Here is another favorite example: I had the fun assignment to talk to 350 Seventh-Day Adventist pastors. The speech was called, "How to Design and Deliver a More Charismatic Sermon." It was the fourth day of a conference and a four-hour seminar. If you go to conferences, you know three days is enough. By the fourth day, you're really ready to go home.

We always have to look at a situation from the point of view of the audience. What would they be thinking? I would expect even the most generous of audience members would be thinking, "Huh, she's the only person on the program who isn't a minister. How can anyone who isn't a minister tell me how to write a better sermon? After all, I write a new one every week. I bet she isn't even a Seventh-Day Adventist," which of course I'm not.

And when you have an audience that doubts your credibility, the absolutely best way to grab credibility in a short period of time is to start with an interesting statistic or little-known fact from their world. I walked out and said, "465 times in the Bible, it said 'It came to pass.' It did not say 'It came to stay.' Unless your sermon is well constructed, artfully crafted, and charismatically delivered, it will not come to stay in the hearts, minds, and lives of your congregation." After that I heard, "Amen! Hallelujah!" and applause. After that moment, I had them hooked.

Good luck with your openings: an original story; a powerful quotation that's not over-used; a rhetorical question; or an interesting statistic or little-known fact.

Final Thoughts

Part of the presence you command on the platform is captured by crafting the right message, choosing the right words, and delivering in the right way. Express yourself with flair, and it will increase the speed with which you succeed!

World Champions' EDGE Testimonial

 *"I am not a professionally paid speaker, but from the training I received from a coaching weekend with Darren and Craig, their excellent materials, and follow-ups I have had with them, I feel like a professional speaker when I get my chance at 'stage time.' Those two words alone make me think twice when I am offered a chance to speak and my first reaction is, 'Oh not this time.' Then Darren's words start throbbing in my mind, and I go for the opportunity.*

I am a member of three Toastmasters clubs because I have greater confidence in myself and my skills, and I know that I need to get up there and tell my story. Talk about a huge return on my investment, I wish my IRA gave me as much of a return as does my membership in the EDGE! Thanks to all of the Champions."

Ron Grusy, South Euclid, Ohio

World Champions' EDGE Testimonial

 *"Champions' EDGE is one of the best ways to enhance your speaking performance and advance your speaking career. Membership within the EDGE has not only provided substantial discounts on resources (Champ Camps) and products (books, DVDs, and MP3s), but more so a community of like-minded speakers and presenters who are serious about their craft.*

The members-only EDGEnet forum and chat room is the epitome of camaraderie. Leave your egos at the door. Members are readily open to share their comments and opinions when asked (and a few times without asking).

With an international gathering that you find on the EDGE, you have access to worldwide resources that are a must if you are serious about the business of speaking or simply wanting to fine-tune that competition speech — all at your fingertips. My time with the EDGE has increased my performance, my pay rate for speaking engagements, and my resource community.

Who do you hang out with — and are they takers or givers?"

Palmo Carpino, Alberta, Canada

CHAPTER 11
The Daily Debrief
How to Be Twice as Good in Seventy Days!

by Ed Tate

Improve 1% everyday and in seventy days, you'll be twice as good. This concept is called the 1% Solution® by best-selling author and consultant, Alan Weiss PhD. By the way, the good people of Massachusetts Institute of Technology (MIT) have confirmed that the math is correct.

A key tool in 1% Solution is the Daily Debrief. In this process, you debrief your performance each day — either alone or with others. Debriefing provides a systematic approach for reflecting on learning experiences. Think of it as evaluation but at a much deeper level.

When asked why people should debrief their performance, educational researcher, instructional designer, and author Sivasailam "Thiagi" Thiagarajan, "People do not learn from experience. They learn from reflecting on their experience. The failure to debrief is the main reason why people fail to reach their full potential in performance."

Debriefing Models

Sales Dogs Debriefing Framework

There are a number of debriefing models. The first debriefing framework comes from Blaire Singer, author of *Sales Dogs: You Do Not Have to Be an Attack Dog to Be Successful in Sales* (www.salesdogs.com). It uses these questions:

- What happened? (list only the facts, no opinions)
- Why?

- What worked?
- What did not work?
- What did you learn?
- What can you do to correct or improve?

Using the Sales Dogs Debriefing Framework, here is how a debriefing might go with one of the clients I coach for speaking.

> **What happened?** "I lost the speech contest."
>
> **Why?** "The judges picked another speaker."
>
> **What worked?** "Humor. I got over a dozen laughs and two laughs were very long."
>
> **What did not work?** "Winning the speech contest!" [After probing further about his performance, my client came up with an additional answer.] "Being authentic or real. My speech was more of a performance than a conversation. I can see that the other speaker did a better job of connecting with the audience."
>
> **What did you learn?** "Not to taking losing so hard. I thought I won based on the number of laughs I got. It's about connecting with the audience."
>
> **What can you do to correct or improve?** "To be real. Focus on connecting with the audience with both my delivery and content. I'm also going to join the Champions' EDGE so I can take advantage of the educational lessons and speech critiques" (learn more about Champions' EDGE in the back of the book)."

Five-Step Framework

Another debriefing framework is from Enlightened Leadership Solutions — the Five-Step Framework (www.elsolutions.com). In this model, the debriefing process uses these questions:

- What's working?
- What caused it to work?
- What is your goal?
- What would be the benefit of achieving this goal?
- What can you do more of or better?

Here is another speech coaching scenario where I might use these questions:

What's working? "Humor"

What caused it to work? "Your audio training program, *Speaking Secrets of the Champions* (visit www.WorldChampionResources.com to learn more). Also, practicing in front of a live audience. I went to multiple Toastmasters clubs to practice my speech."

What is your goal? "To win the speech contest, become a better speaker, and connect with audiences every time."

What would be the benefit of achieving this goal? "Improved confidence."

What can you do more of or better? "Focus more on connecting with audiences in future speeches."

Alignment Dynamics Debrief Form

A good friend of mine, Kevin Spalding of Alignment Dynamics, Inc. (www.alignment-dynamics.com) has created a daily debrief form that is shown on the next page. Like the others, it asks what worked and what didn't and why. It goes further and also tracks other key activities necessary for a successful professional such as networking, training, reading, and material development. It even tracks progress in all quadrants of your life such as personal, physical, spiritual, and family.

Final Thoughts

These are three of the many debriefing models. If you follow Alan Weiss' 1% Solution and utilize a daily debrief, you'll be twice as good in seventy days. And the applications are not just limited to speaking or training. I apply the daily debrief to all aspects of my professional and personal life. What would happen if you applied this concept of a daily debrief to all areas of you life? How much better would your speaking be? Imagine how much better your personal relationships would be as well. All it takes is asking a few reflective questions each day.

ALIGNING ENERGIES
ALIGNMENT DYNAMICS, INC.
FOCUSED FOR RESULTS

Daily Debrief Form

Date: _____

Overall

_____

_____

Business

_____ Calls Made   _____ Appointments Made

_____ Appointments Kept   _____ Follow-ups

Networking_____

Presentations Made _____

Training/Reading _____

_____

Material Development_____

_____

Other _____

_____

What worked? _____

Why? _____

What didn't work?_____

Why? _____

Personal

_____

_____

_____

Physical

_____

_____

_____

Spiritual

_____

_____

_____

Family

_____

_____

_____

General and Priorities for Tomorrow

_____

_____

_____

World Champions' EDGE Testimonial

 *"If you're serious about taking your speaking skills to great heights, you'll invest in the EDGE — no, you'll invest in YOURSELF. I've been a member from the inception. My results could fill this book, but here are just a few:*

- Incorporating just one technique from the monthly audio lesson had the women in my audience at a recent keynote 'eating out of my hand.' Because of the success, the meeting planner couldn't wait to book me again. You get great ideas every month!

- Access to the Champs is enabling me to re-brand my speaking and training business without making costly errors.

- Finding reputable vendors and resources can be overwhelming and risky but the Champs know the who, what, and where to go to. You can't beat having access to those resources. As a result, I now have a cost-effective, professional-looking banner that showcases my speaking.

- Best of all, you get discounts to the Champs' educational events with your membership. Once you've been to one and had their hands-on coaching, you won't regret it. I have my first, but not last, CD as a result of this experience.

Do yourself a favor this year, and join the EDGE. You'll be glad you did!"

Kay Fittes, Cincinnati, Ohio

CHAPTER 12
Four Ways to Tighten Up Your Speech

by Craig Valentine

One of the biggest problems presenters make is giving speeches that are too loose. When I say loose, I mean their content is not tied to anything. It results in a message that is not memorable or meaningful. As a result, they see audience members shifting uncomfortably in their seats and feel like they are losing them with every word.

The solution is to tie every major point you make in your speech to an anchor of some sort. An anchor is anything that helps audience members remember your points. In other words, when they think back to your anchor, they automatically recall the message that accompanies it. When a non-attendee asks your audience members what you talked about, your message will be at the front of their brains.

Here are four major anchors you can use to make your speech stick. I call them the Four As for Anchors.

Anecdotes (Stories)

By far, the greatest way to anchor a point is with a story. In addition to being memorable, stories also evoke emotions that get your audience to not only hear your speech but also to feel it. Surely you still remember the childhood stories such as *The Boy Who Cried Wolf* or even *The Wizard of Oz*. When you remember these stories, you immediately recall the messages (lessons) that were attached to them.

Activities

Think back to a class or workshop that included an activity. Can you remember the point the activity made? When done well, activities not only act as anchors, they also re-energize your audience in the process.

Analogies

I regularly use the old classic metaphor of the crabs in a barrel (pulling each other down as they try to get out) to explain what happens when you hang around negative people. When my audience thinks of the crabs in a barrel, they remember to be careful who they keep close to them. The key is to compare something your audience knows (or can picture) to something they do not yet understand. There is an old saying that a picture is worth a thousand words but a metaphor is worth a thousand pictures. They are that powerful!

Acronyms

In a workshop I gave recently, I used the acronym PARTS to teach a formula for creating captivating content in a speech. Acronyms work well because they present a built-in sequence that is easy for your audience to follow. For example, my audience knows after I finish with P (which stands for Phrase), I will move on to the A. When your audience knows your road map, your speech becomes tighter to them and is easier to remember.

Final Thoughts

When your audience members think back on any of these anchors, they automatically remember the points that are attached. A great way to make sure your message sticks is to mix multiple anchors within one speech. I regularly use all four of them in a forty-five-minute speech. The idea is to simply move from one anchor to the next. Using a good mix of anchors keeps your audience energized, and they walk away with a message that they can grasp with ease. Always tie your content to these anchors, and you will forever keep your speech tight.

World Champions' EDGE Testimonial

"I know that I definitely would not be where I am today without the EDGE support network."

Jo Nell Fulwiler, Professional Storyteller, Plano, Texas

World Champions' EDGE Testimonial

 *"Last year I achieved my dream of becoming one of the ten finalists in Toastmaster's World Championship of Public Speaking. I could not have done it without World Champions' EDGE. The genesis of all three of my speeches — district, regional, and international — was attending the Champ Camps. Throughout the contest cycle, the speeches were critiqued a number of times by different Champs who provided valuable and unique insights into speech writing, development, and delivery. All of the principals of World Champions' EDGE have been my mentors and have become my friends. I thank them for the ride of my life!"*

Charlie Wilson, State College, Pennsylvania

CHAPTER 13
Lights ...
Camera ...
H U M O R!
Comedy Secrets for
Professional Presentations

by Darren LaCroix

You're watching someone else's presentation, and they're getting laughs! It looks easy, so you ask yourself, "How can I do that?" What do some presenters know that others don't? It's simple — they know the secrets from the comedy world!

When you see a comedian on television, what you see looks easy. What you don't see is all of the work it took to make it look easy. They probably performed that same five-minute routine for seven nights in a row at two comedy shows per night. Never mind the years of experience as well. Don't beat yourself up if you have a hard time being as funny as the comedy pros!

Besides practice, the other advantage is they know comedy principles. Since I started doing stand-up comedy back in 1992, this was the biggest revelation. There are actually comedy-writing exercises that comedians use. This was huge eye-opener for me because I was not naturally funny, but I was willing to do my homework to learn to get the laughs. We all need to be a "student of humor." I'm still learning myself.

Are you ready for a simple secret that you can use in your next presentation? Fellow students of humor: stand up and make 'em laugh! As I teach others and make techniques and concepts graspable, I, too, gain more clarity. I'm still on my own ever-changing path of humor mastery.

Rule of Three

If you have heard me speak in person, you know that one of my favorite things to teach is the Rule of Three — with a humor twist. It's just one of the ideas we teach at the Humor Boot Camp® (www.humorbootcamp.com). You may be aware that in professional presentations, a "list of three" is often used to illustrate examples. For instance, in my observations about happiness, I talk about the excuses we all make. We would be happier IF …

> "If I just had a little more money … If I just had a little more time … If the kids were just a little older …"

Three illustrations are optimum because two may not give full clarity or allow the audience to recognize themselves. Four items seems to belabor the point. Unless it is an unusually difficult concept to grasp, no one likes it when people overdo an explanation.

This concept works very well with the "setup/punch" format and anyone can develop the technique. The setup creates an expectation. The punch line changes that expectation. We can use the Rule of Three to develop a pattern. Establishing the pattern then allows for us to break the pattern, and that's where we get the laugh!

I was giving a humor workshop in Sarasota, Florida, so I scheduled an appearance at a comedy club in town that same night. Some of the attendees mentioned that they were coming to the show. I decided to challenge myself and create a local joke based on the Rule of Three so they could see it in action. My friend, Elizabeth, one of the attendees, worked through the process with me. Here is how I started the show:

> "I'm excited to be visiting Sarasota. My friends were delighted to show me the local wildlife. They took me to see the dolphins at Miaka, the alligators at Sonata Island, and the drivers on Route 41."

Notice the pattern: AB AB AB. A pattern needs to be created in order to change the expectation. "A" was the location. "B" was an animal. Notice that the "wildlife" got progressively wilder. That's why I started with dolphins rather than alligators.

See how it works? In the setup, you create a pattern, so the pattern creates an expectation. Then the expectation is your setup for a nice humorous twist.

But how is an idea created? What creative process do you use? Humor often stems from tragedy. I started by asking about some of the common local complaints. One thing that screamed out from the top of the "pet peeve" list was the drivers. You usually don't have to look very far for comedy!

Local drivers were going to be my punch line. Now I went back and looked at how I could hide the punch line and set up the joke. Noticing that there were many vacationers in Sarasota, the idea of vacations seemed like a logical way to hide the punch line.

A Great Example from a Student of Humor

For a recent speech in Montreal, John Gupta, Distinguished Toastmaster and Past District Governor for Toastmasters was introducing me. He used the Rule of Three that I had taught him at a previous conference. He actually put an added twist on it:

> "When people find out that I'm Indian, they think I practice yoga, I meditate, and I'm poor. [pause] The third one is correct!"

He used a *1, 2, 3 … then BANG* formula. It was very funny! What John did was use an unfortunate stereotype to his advantage. He can get away with it because he is talking about himself. At the same time, he loosened up the audience, showed that he takes himself lightly, and set a creative tone for his presentation. The magic was that he did all of that in just twenty-three words. Brilliant! I love seeing someone use what I teach. It works, yet most people will not even attempt it.

The greatest benefit to his creation is that he can use it whenever he speaks to an audience. A little effort goes a long way. John can use this bit for many years to come. It is a nice icebreaker.

Looking into Personal Experience to Find the Moments of Humor

If you'd been sitting in the front row at a Champions' EDGE Summit (our biannual members-only event), you would've heard me say something that had never come out of my mouth before! As soon as the words left my mouth, fellow World Champion of Public Speaking for Toastmasters International, Craig Valentine, said, "That was gold!"

Wow! What did I say?

Sometimes if we're speaking from our heart, we have moments of brilliance that we overlook. Sometimes we only notice them when we see the reactions of our audience members. As presenters, we need to capture these moments, and make sure we continue to deliver them in our future presentations. This is one powerful reason to record your presentation every time!

Here's what happened: I was sharing the stage with Mark Brown and Craig Valentine, the 1995 and 1999 World Champions of Public Speaking. We were talking about how to add humor to a speech. I mentioned a brilliant quote by Craig, "Don't add humor. Instead, uncover it." Too many speakers say, "My speech is done, I just need to add humor." To do that is truly like squeezing a square peg into a round hole. The audience will notice how artificial it is.

Mark, who was my coach when I was competing in 2001, mentioned to the EDGE Members that when I was working on my championship speech, I drove two and a half hours each way to work with him — twice. This prompted a memory of my "process."

In 2001, I struggled to find an idea for my speech. We had come to a standstill. After one of the run-throughs of my speech, Mark asked if I had any other stories that might fit.

I hesitated, "Well, I do have this one joke I used to tell years ago when doing stand-up comedy." Mark said, "Let's try it."

So, I told my famous "doubled my debt" joke — although it was not so famous at the time. Mark's chin — and pen — dropped. "That's perfect!" he said.

"Really?" I replied. Because of his years of speaker coaching, Mark saw something that I didn't. I did not understand why he was so excited.

The joke was delivered with an overconfident air: "After four years of business school, I went for the American Dream. I bought a sandwich shop. I don't want to brag, but I took a $60,000 debt, and in just six months, I doubled that debt. That's right, I turned my Subway into a non-profit organization."

After years of coaching other speakers, I can now see what Mark saw. It's quite simple and obvious. My "doubled my debt" joke was based on a true experience from a personal story.

At the EDGE Summit that day, here's what I said, and how I summed up that story:

> "I didn't add humor to my speech. Instead, I uncovered a concise personal story that was relevant to my main message."

This may sound obvious, but if it's so obvious, why do so few presenters use it? Why didn't I ever understand this self-effacing joke when I was writing my speech so long ago?

Will you record yourself to capture your own brilliant moments? Will you search for your own funny, concise personal stories relevant to your main message?

Sharpen Your EDGE

1. Make a long list (at least twenty items) on any topic — then pick the three with the most impact to use with the Rule of Three.

2. Make a list of highlights from your own background and the stereotypes that are connected to it.
   - Your own nationality (French, Polish, etc.)
   - Your serious hobbies (movies, disc golf, etc.)
   - Your jobs (telemarketer, shoe salesman, etc.)

3. Go through your story file — twice. First, list the points you can make that each story might support. Then, go through the stories again. This time, watch for the moments of humor you can uncover.

World Champions' EDGE Testimonial

"You helped me to see how important my message on drugs is for audiences to hear, and you instilled the belief that I can really change lives with my speaking."

Bonnie Laabs, Grove City, Minnesota

Winning Techniques

CHAPTER 14

Using Plan B Can Make Your Presentation Stand Out

by Darren LaCroix

Have you ever sat though a boring presentation? Ever given one? Do you think the presenter actually planned to be boring? Did you? If you answered "Yes!" and then "No!" to these questions, it's time to try my Plan B.

I've given keynote presentations around the world. And no matter if I am speaking in Oman, Malaysia, or Taiwan, ninety-nine percent of the time, there are speakers before me. So I begin my presentation by telling the audience, "Just want you to know that for my presentation, there will be … no slides! Eight hundred and forty-two slides so far … I counted!"

Inevitably, the audience bursts into applause. Why? Because they are tired of looking at slide after slide after slide after … you get the idea.

Too many presenters have forgotten the meaning of "presentation aid." An aid should further the message, support it, assist it … but not be the message.

Slide shows have become the Band-Aid to cover the wound of poor presentation preparation. The people who say, "I don't have time to prepare my presentation so *my plan* is to just refer to my slides," are the people who throw the slides together the night before. Instead of referring to the slides, they read them. Doesn't that make you want to stand up and yell, "I can read! Why not just send me a copy of the slides and save my time!" (Unless, of course, you needed a nap!)

And here's my biggest pet peeve: the final slide that says "Thank you." What? You needed help saying thank you? Shut off the slides, and talk to me! Isn't that what a presentation is about?

Slides, actually, are quite helpful if the presenter remembers to do one thing: talk to the audience. A presenter is there to educate, inspire, and persuade.

Now you're probably thinking, "Okay, Darren, point made. So what's this Plan B you mentioned?"

Here is Plan B: Do you know the most powerful key on your keyboard? It's the "B" key. During a slide presentation, if you hit the B key, the screen goes black. Think about that. In the middle of your presentation, you have the ability to make your screen go black. Do not let the simplicity overshadow its power.

In addition to giving keynote speeches for a living, I also coach CEOs and executives in this skill. One of my corporate clients is a group of account executives from an Internet company. They give sales presentations for six-figure contracts. Presentations are crucial to their bottom line and their individual careers.

In the coaching sessions, each executive gives a five-minute presentation that is then critiqued. During one particular session, I gave an assignment to find one place in which to use the B key. They needed to find a logical place to make the screen go black and to just speak directly to the audience. The goal was to make a compelling point or to tell a client success story, and then hit the B key again and return to the slides.

When the first person finished, I looked around the room and asked, "Did you notice a difference?" The executives were stunned! Their faces said it all.

Powerful presentations are ones in which presenters connect with the audience through the power of their words — the power of their delivery. You cannot persuade anyone when you are looking at slides instead of the audience.

Final Thoughts

Don't let the slide show get in your way. The next time you are giving a slide presentation, remember Plan B: Open strong (with a black screen), close strong (with a black screen), and find one place in the middle where you speak directly to the audience with a black screen behind you. It will be powerful!

World Champions' EDGE Testimonial

"*I enjoy the wealth of interesting and helpful information on your website. I listen to the EDGE CDs every day in my car. I am a realtor and therefore spend a great deal of time driving. I have listened and re-listened to more than one of your CDs. I find my membership very valuable. I gain a great deal from the experiences you so willingly share. Thanks to each of you for your input, ideas, and tips for improving my speeches.*"

Iris Talbot, Realtor, Alberta, Canada

CHAPTER 15
The Suspended Story

by Mark Brown

Many effective speeches follow a pattern that I like to describe as "going full circle." This is best defined as a presentation in which the beginning of the speech is tied to its conclusion. All that takes place in between — the points made, the examples given, the concepts shared — guides the listeners on a journey which ends with a clearly defined connection to the opening. There is a technique that makes the concept of going full circle more memorable. It's called "The Suspended Story." The method is quite simple.

Very early in the speech, tell a story that grabs and holds the audience's attention, gets them engaged, and leaves them in suspense. As you near the climactic end of the story, suspend the telling of the tale, and segue smoothly into the "weightier" material in your speech. This will create the "cliff-hanger" effect that will keep the audience in suspense. However, you must commit to resolving the conflict that you have created and to revealing the remainder of the story at the end of your presentation, thereby completing the circle. Here is a note of caution: at best, this is a risky proposition. Here are guidelines for using this technique effectively.

Select Your Story Very Carefully

You may have a favorite story — one that you enjoy telling and one that has been well received by previous audiences. However, that story may not be appropriate for use in this manner. It may not be ripe for suspension. You have to be certain that the story you select fits the theme of your presentation. Don't give in to the temptation to use a story just because you like telling it.

Your story should have three basic components:

- **Suspense or drama:** Relying on the setup line for a joke may not be the best option. While the setup could have suspense attached, it may not necessarily create enough suspense or be weighty enough to bear the burden of the subsequent points you wish to make.

- **Brevity:** If the story is too long, key elements might be forgotten by the time you get to the conclusion of your speech.

- **Simplicity:** The story should be very easy to follow. A multi-layered story could complicate the message and confuse the audience. It could also give them too much to think about and too much to remember.

Use the Technique Sparingly

Please don't use this technique arbitrarily. It is best not to make this a part of your regular speech format. The suspended story is a dramatic change from what an audience might expect and — when used properly — will catch the audience off guard, leaving them wanting to hear how the story is resolved. Here is an example:

> "My friend Bob, an entrepreneur from New Jersey, made plans to attend a meeting in Portland. Attendees were flying in from cities across the USA to attend the event. An extremely frugal individual, Bob always searches for the best deals on hotels, rental cars, and airline tickets. He was overjoyed to learn that he was able to secure flights at rates that were more than $300 lower than he had anticipated. On the day of his flight, he arrived at the airport with ninety minutes to spare. He checked his e-mail, bought some coffee and a newspaper, and calmly waited for his flight to be called. At boarding time, he approached the jetway and was met by a friendly gate agent who commented that she was a bit envious of him. "Why?" asked Bob, to which the agent replied, "What I wouldn't give to visit the beautiful seaport town of Portland right now. Maine has the most beautiful fall colors at this time of year!" Bob listened courteously and then stopped short as a thought crossed his mind. That thought is exactly what I will share with you at the end of my presentation!"

At this point, the story is suspended. But the material to follow must be directly related to the story as told so far and must be reinforced at the end when the story is resolved.

In this example, the speech could then focus on the value of effective communication skills. Let's continue.

> "Aha! Now maybe you're thinking, 'Hey! That's not fair!' But you're THINKING and that's important! I'd like you to THINK about what goes through YOUR mind when you engage others in conversation. Are you an effective speaker, listener, and communicator?"

It would then be very easy for me to discuss the various components of effective communication, using as much detail as was necessary. As I approach the end of my presentation, I could focus on the value of listening and gathering information as critical aspects of communication. This would then lead me to seamlessly "going full circle." Here is a possible conclusion:

> "All too often, when in conversation, we don't listen carefully enough. We're prone to thinking about what we will say next, and we don't pay close attention to what others are saying. Sadly, all too often, we miss valuable and sometimes critical information. And that's what happened to Bob. As he stood there about to board his flight, the thought hit him. 'Yes, Portland, Maine is a vision of splendor in the fall. But my conference is in Portland, OREGON, and I'll never get there in time! No wonder the tickets were so cheap! How could I have missed that?' The stark realization that he would have to take a flight the next day and fly for five hours instead of one only magnified his anguish. Like Bob, we miss so much by not speaking clearly, listening keenly, and thinking things through. Remember to make sure that you are clearly understood, make sure that your listeners understand your meaning, and always THINK before you speak or act. It can make a world of difference, but more importantly, so will YOU!"

That is but one example of how the suspended story could be used effectively. In the example above, I could have suspended the story even more dramatically by adding a single word like sickening, terrifying, or mortifying, and then suspending the story. I could also steer the presentation along a slightly different path. Here's what I mean.

> "Bob listened courteously, and then stopped short as a terrifying thought crossed his mind! Can you recall a time in your life when you were stopped short by a terrifying thought? I can! Terrifying

thoughts bombard us constantly, and our thoughts determine how we act, how we respond, and how we face life's daily challenges. Charles Reade is quoted as saying, 'Sow a thought, and you reap an act; sow an act, and you reap a habit; sow a habit, and you reap a character; sow a character, and you reap a destiny.' What thoughts are you sowing every day? How are you shaping your destiny?"

With just a slight adjustment to the language, the suspended story can lead to a discussion about the power of our thoughts and their effect on our lives. Choices abound, and you must select that which bests suits your objectives.

Final Thoughts

Remember that the suspended story can enhance your speech, insert the element of suspense, and help you to take your presentation full circle. Just remember to choose your story carefully and use the technique sparingly.

World Champions' EDGE Testimonial

 *"I received feedback that my class was inspiring, that I was phenomenal, and I was asked if I would speak outside the Learning Annex. I just want to thank you and let you know that your teachings DO work."*

Isaak Gelbinovich, Staten Island, New York

World Champions' EDGE Testimonial

 *"I am impressed how the response to my joining was so immediate. I received two EDGEucational CDs in just two days. I began receiving the weekly audio list right away. I also downloaded two of the items available to download. I found one passage in one of the CDs to be of immediate use. I can see how this membership will help me achieve goals as a professional speaker. I recommend joining to anybody in this field."*

Marvin Petsel, Plano, Texas

CHAPTER 16
Tap and Transport
The Two Ts to Terrific Teaching

by Craig Valentine

Whether you are a teacher, trainer, or speaker, there are two methods you can use to teach at the highest level. I taught middle school for a couple of years, ran a basketball camp for kids for several years, and I have been teaching and training adults regularly since 1999. But more importantly, as I study other teachers, trainers, and speakers, I find that the most effective ones use a two-T process (Tap and Transport) even if they are not completely conscious of it.

This process will allow you to connect better with your audience, and they will buy in to your message more deeply. People buy in to what they help create, and the Tap and Transport process makes them part of the learning process.

Tap: The Key to Hooking Your Audience

Tap into their world first before you ask them to come into yours. In education, "tap" may be expressed as "activating prior knowledge." It means to discover what your audience already knows about a certain topic before you dive into that topic. Effective teachers know that activating prior knowledge helps students organize their new information.

For example, an eighth-grade teacher who is teaching today's students about the civil rights movement in the 1950s and 1960s might begin a lesson by asking, "Have you ever felt like someone was not being fair to you? How did you react? What were you feeling? What do you think would be an appropriate way to handle your situation?"

Now, once the students successfully reflect on their own experiences, the teacher can easily segue into her material like this: "Well, come with me to Montgomery, Alabama on a hot, muggy day in 1956. We are watching hundreds of people walk to work as the empty buses go by. Do you know why there aren't any people on the buses?"

Now she will have much more buy-in from the students because they can relate to the feelings of the people who felt they were treated unfairly. With this new perspective, being treated unfairly is much more relevant and real to the students because the teacher tapped into their world first before taking them somewhere else.

When you tap and activate that prior knowledge, you make it much easier for your audience members to relate what they already know to what they are about to learn. A side benefit is that you get your audience to actually think in the process. My speech coach, Patricia Fripp, said to me, "Craig, wisdom comes from reflection." The more we provoke our audience to think, the more likely they are to retain the information. Take a look at how I use the tap process to help one of my management audiences reflect:

> "Do you know any StatusQuoaholics? You know, these are the kind of people who are averse to change. They say things like, 'This is the way we've always done things. Why change?' Do you know anyone like this? What do they do to your team? What if you could change even the most reluctant statusquoaholic into a force for change? If you had been in my office in East Baltimore about fifty yards from the city jail, you would have witnessed an event that got out of hand …"

Now that I have tapped into their world with some relevant questions that stirred up their emotions, I can rest assured that they are thinking about themselves as I move to the second part of the process.

Transport: Invite Your Audience to Join You on Your Journey

Now that you know how to tap, let's move to the next step: transport. Notice from the example above that you didn't just receive a question — you were transported to another scene. Being able to transport your audience is one of the most important skills you can have as a speaker, and unfortunately, it is one of the most neglected.

Too many speakers give too little thought to these all-important make-or-break moments in their speeches. Here is the way many speakers make a failed attempt to transport their audience members into a story.

> "I would like to tell you a story about blah blah blah," or "Once upon a time back in 1964, I ..."

As a speaker, you should not force yourself out into your audience. Rather, you should invite your audience to come to you and with you.

Here is what you should understand about transporting your audience into a story: make it you-focused. For example, don't say, "I would like to tell a story about so and so." Instead, invite them to the scene. A couple sentences may make all the difference. Here is an example of how I might transport and invite you into one of my scenes.

> "If you had been sitting beside my wife and me on our old black leather sofa, with the chocolate chip cookies baking in the background, you would have heard her say something that can absolutely change your life. I know it changed mine."

Tools That Invite Your Audience into Your Scene

Use your creativity to invite audience members to your scene. This is one of my favorite parts of any speech because there are so many ways to transport them there. In this story, I said, "If you were sitting beside my wife and me." Sometimes, in other stories, I may say, "You should have been with me as I ..."

Here is the key that makes this successful: put your audience somewhere in your scene. Whether you put them on the sofa next to you and your spouse, ask them to walk with you into a doctor's office, or have them pick up your phone (as in "If you had picked up my phone in the year 2000 ..."), you should put them somewhere in your scene so they can watch it unfold. Relive the story, and invite your audience into your "reliving" room.

Check the VAKS

Once you bring them into your scene, follow it up with the VAKS (Visual, Auditory, Kinesthetic, and Smell) formula. By the way, I know "smell" is technically "olfactory" but "Check the VAKO" does not have the same ring to it.

So let's go back to the sofa with my wife and me, and let's list the VAKS.

- What could you see (visual)? You could see the black leather sofa.
- What could you hear (auditory)? You could hear my wife.
- What could you feel (kinesthetic)? You could feel the love and probably the leather.
- What could you smell? You could smell the chocolate chip cookies. You could probably taste them too.

Final Thoughts

When you transport your audience into your story, check all the VAKS conscientiously. Take this part of your speech seriously. You will find your audience members look at you as if they are actually with you as you revisit and relive the scenes in your stories.

This is a connection that will not happen by accident. It comes from purposeful planning and the use of the Tap and Transport formula. Remember to engage the Two Ts to Terrific Teaching — tap and transport — before you teach.

World Champions' EDGE Testimonial

"You don't know how much being part of World Champions' EDGE has helped me personally and professionally. I owe my new job with a 20-percent increase in base pay to my involvement with Toastmasters and connecting with the Champs and Patricia Fripp."

Bill Kennedy, Central Islip, New York

World Champions' EDGE Testimonial

 *"Not long after joining Champion's EDGE, I won the Toastmasters International Speech Contest at my club in London in 2008. Whilst I didn't win the next round, I experienced a huge leap in my development as a speaker. For me, that was more important and longer lasting than an award. I got feedback on my speech from some fellow EDGE members and had the opportunity to give it again at a workshop later. Again, I experienced another spike in my development. My progress was both rapid and breathtaking.*

I'm normally skeptical buying things over the Internet, but I am so glad that I took a risk. This has to be one of the best investments I've ever made.

If you're looking for an edge in your next presentation — a real edge — you should invest in yourself and join Champions' EDGE. It's like having the home telephone numbers of former World Champion of Public Speaking on speed dial."

Jason Peck, Humorist and Speaker, London, England

CHAPTER 17

It's Easier to Earn a Gold Medal Than to Win a Trophy!

What Are You Doing to Choose the Special Event That Will Define Your Life?

by Ed Tate

It's called a *palindrome* — a number or word that reads the same backward and forward. One example of a palindrome is 08-08-08 — August 8, 2008. It's a rare occurrence on a calendar. Around the world, August of 2008 was filled with rare occurrences.

One such occurrence took place in Beijing, People's Republic of China. The games of the 29th Olympiad began on 08-08-08 at 8:08 p.m. with 10,500 athletes competing in 302 events. Gold medals were awarded in twenty-eight sports.

On August 16, 2008, another rare occurrence happened in Calgary, Alberta, Canada. The "Olympics of Oratory" was held — Toastmasters International's World Championship of Public Speaking competition. Over 230,000 Toastmasters members from ninety-two countries compete in this nine-month, six-round contest. In the grand finale of this annual competition that showcases the ten finalists, only one trophy is awarded. In 2008, the trophy was awarded to LaShunda Rundles of Dallas, Texas.

Let's assume that the number of contestants were equal for both events — 10,500 each for the Olympics and the World Championship of Public Speaking (WCPS). Statistically, a contestant has a better chance of winning one of the 302 gold medals than a single Toastmasters World Championship trophy — 302 to 1.

You are probably saying to yourself, "This is not a fair comparison. You can't compare athletes to speakers." And you'd be right. It's like comparing apples to oranges. So let's compare speakers to speakers.

On August 5, 2008, another rare occasion took place in New York City. The National Speakers Association (NSA) and the International Federation for Professional Speakers awarded forty-one speakers with gold medals for speaking excellence — the Certified Speaking Professional designation. This is proof in the arena of public speaking that you have a better chance of winning a gold medal than you do a Toastmasters trophy. In the case of the 2008 ceremony, the odds were 41 to 1.

Everyone who is serious and dedicated about being a professional speaker can earn this gold medal. The National Speakers Association established the Certified Speaking Professional (CSP) designation in 1980. It is the speaking industry's international measure of professional platform skill. The CSP is granted only to those who have earned it by meeting strict criteria. When the letters "CSP" follow a speaker's name, it indicates that individual is a competent speaking professional with proven experience who understands what is required and knows how to deliver client satisfaction.

Even though it's easier to win the CSP gold medal than a World Champion of Public Speaking trophy, fewer than ten percent of the 4,700 speakers who belong to the National Speakers Association or the International Federation for Professional Speakers hold this professional designation. Even though it is more accessible, few make the effort to earn it.

I have won both — the gold medal and the trophy. On August 5, 2008, I was among the class of forty-one CSP recipients. And on August 26, 2000, I won the Toastmasters World Championship of Public Speaking trophy. In fact, I'm one of the few people in the world who has won both.

Every year, hundreds of people from around the world approach me about helping them win the World Championship of Public Speaking trophy. However, I think they should go for the gold instead — the CSP gold medal.

Here's why: I'm happy to have earned the CSP and won the WCPS. I value them both equally but for different reasons. Winning the WCPS has been a life-altering event. Because of the speaking invitations I've received, I've been around the world five times. The title boosted my speaking career. It inspired me to pursue speaking as a profession. And it is still paying benefits and providing unique experiences today. For example, a camera crew followed several previous World Champions of Public Speaking around in Calgary at the 2008 Toastmasters International Convention to film a documentary about Toastmasters. I got a chance to be part of that documentary.

Allow me to explain what winning this honor is not. It is not a guarantee to fame. Outside of the Toastmasters world, very few people know who I am.

It is also not a guarantee to fortune. When I won, I got all the free speech offers a person could handle. In fact, I did not get one paid speech offer. Because of my business background and marketing acumen that I developed along the way, I was able to get paid for speaking eventually. It took a lot of hard work and effort on my part to make this happen. I did not quit my day job for eighteen months after winning the contest.

And if I had to do it again, I would have waited an additional eighteen months. Public speaking is a great permanent part-time job forever. You never have to quit your day job. Unfortunately, many people quit their day jobs to pursue this professional speaking passion only to bankrupt themselves.

Let's look closer at the gold medal — the CSP. It took me over nine years to earn this designation. Speakers can be eligible in as little as five years if they make it part of their goals at the beginning of their speaking career and collect the proper documentation along the way. Like the World Championship of Public Speaking, outside of the speaking industry, it has very little recognition. However, inside the industry, CSPs are recognized as one of the best speakers in the business and have a proven track record. Since I earned my CSP, speaker bureaus are now taking my calls and booking me.

Final Thoughts

Here is the point I want you to remember: Only one person a year can win the World Championship of Public Speaking. However, every person reading this book can earn their CSP. Every one of you who is serious about a career as a professional speaker can earn their CSP. The first step is to join the National Speakers Association or the International Federation for Professional Speakers. Developing platform excellence at delivering a compelling topic in a way that yields satisfied clients is also part of the process. Another step is running your business in a way that provides a steady stream of paid speaking engagements.

Everyone can be a winner. To learn more about becoming a CSP, go to www.nsaspeaker.org for the technical qualifications.

World Champions' EDGE Testimonial

"This is truly amazing! The value you give in the EDGE seriously exceeds the price. If anybody ever wants to improve their speaking in any capacity, they need to get the EDGE – yesterday!"

Frederic Gray, Temple Terrace, Florida

World Champions' EDGE Testimonial

"Since being a member and receiving the weekly audio lessons, I have become a better coach to my own students. Although I am far away in New Zealand, I feel like I have my own personal team behind me all the way. Their amazing tips and advice have helped so much in building my own strategies in teaching the spoken word.

Thank you David, Craig, Ed, Darren, Mark, and the lady in the group, Patricia. I have also now received my Gold Speaker Award, and with your input as well, I have been able to develop more opportunities for coaching younger students."

Anna Stonnell, Hamilton, New Zealand

CHAPTER 18

Earning Credibility That Wins Business

Present Your Proposal at an Executive Meeting and Sell Your Way to Success

by Patricia Fripp

What's the worst reaction you've ever gotten when you made an important presentation? Probably, it would come in second to the one I just heard about. A woman — ironically she was interviewing me for an article called "Knockout Presentations" — told me the story of her disaster.

It was early in her career as a policy analyst. She was just out of school, proud of her MBA, and working in her first real job. When her supervisor praised a report she'd done, she was thrilled. She was less thrilled when her reward for a job well done turned out to be presenting the same report to their executive team.

She spent a tense week getting ready, making sure she knew exactly what to say. She spent hours writing out her presentation and prepared every conceivable statistic to back up her points. It never occurred to her, however, that *how* she presented was as important as *what* she presented.

When her turn came to deliver her report, things quickly went downhill. Naturally, she was nervous. A lot depended on the next few minutes. She stumbled through 200 slides, forgot her lines, and got more and more flustered. Bored executives weren't sure what her point was and started glancing at their watches, which made it even worse. Desperate, she wanted to flee — and her audience probably did too! When she concluded, they didn't ask a single question. That would have extended the already painful event.

Does any of this sound familiar to you? If not, great! And let's make sure it never does — especially if a lot depends on how well you do. You probably know that the higher up the corporate ladder you go, the more important your communication skills become. And the faster you develop and hone your skills, the faster you'll climb.

Perhaps you're already speaking up in team meetings and getting your ideas across effectively. If so, how do you feel about facing a room full of senior managers — or at least five around a boardroom table — all staring at you? What is different? Well, for one thing, the stakes are higher.

All business communications are important; but with senior management as your audience, you are in the hot seat. They are going to accept or reject the recommendations that you, your department, or your team have worked so hard on. Weeks, months, maybe even years of work depend on your few minutes. Who wouldn't be nervous?

Don't worry. You are human. This is a perfectly natural way to feel. Remember, they can't see how you feel. Only how you look and act are visible to your audience. You want them to focus on and consider your proposals, not your anxiety. And you'll look cool and collected when you follow these Frippicisms for dealing with senior management.

Seven Fripp Do's

- **Practice.** A report to senior managers is not a conversation; however, it must sound conversational. Once you have your notes, practice by speaking out loud to an associate, when you are driving to work, or on the treadmill. Make sure you are familiar with what you intend to say. It is not about being *perfect* — it is about being *personable*. Remember, rehearsal is the work; performance is the relaxation.

- **Open with your conclusions.** Don't make your senior-level audience wait to find out why you are there.

- **Describe the benefits if your recommendation is adopted.** Make these benefits seem vivid and obtainable.

- **Describe the costs, but frame them in a positive manner.** If possible, show how not following your recommendation will cost even more.

- **List your specific recommendations, and keep it on target.** Wandering generalities will lose their interest. You must focus on the bottom line. Report on the deals, not the details.

- **Look everyone in the eye when you talk.** You will be more persuasive and believable. You can't do this if you are reading, so you must know your material well!

- **Be brief.** The fewer words you can use to get your message across, the better. Jerry Seinfeld says, "I spend an hour taking an eight-word sentence and making it five." That's because he knew it would be funnier. In your case, shorter is more memorable and repeatable.

Three Fripp Don'ts

- **Don't try to memorize the whole presentation.** Memorize your opening, key points, and conclusion. Practice enough so you can "forget it." This helps retain your spontaneity.

- **Never, never read your lines** — not from a script and not from PowerPoint® slides. Your audience will go to sleep.

- **Don't wave or hop.** Don't let nervousness (or enthusiasm) make you too animated but don't freeze. Unnecessary movement can distract your audience from your own message.

Every Great Proposal Starts with Great Questions

Regardless of how important you believe your topic is, you will encounter people who need a little help buying in. If you are able to put yourself in the seats around the boardroom table and ask some questions, it will set you up for greater success. The best way to do that is to ask questions that will help you design your message to meet their unique interests and needs.

Ask yourself these three questions:

- What is the topic or subject you are reporting on? Be clear with yourself so you can be clear with your audience.

- Why is your topic important enough to be on the busy agenda of senior-level managers?

- What questions will your audience ask? Can you answer them early in your presentation?

Creating a Successful Proposal

Here is an example of a process that you can use to create a winning proposal.

Present Your Conclusion

What is your central theme, objective, or the big idea of your report? How can you introduce it in one sentence? Suppose that you've been in charge of a high-level, cross-functional team to study whether there is a need for diversity training in your company. You might start by saying, "Our committee has spent three months studying diversity training programs and whether one could benefit our company. Our conclusion is that diversity training would be an exceptionally good investment. We would save money, increase employee retention, and improve company morale."

Present Your Recommendations

"We recommend that the company initiate a pilot program, starting next quarter, using the ABC Training Company at an investment of $_____. The ABC Company has successfully implemented this program with one of our subsidiaries as well as many Fortune 100 companies. All twenty-seven members of the cross-functional team agreed with this conclusion. Our team was made up of a cross-section of the company — two vice presidents, the facilities department secretary, eighteen associates (some with PhDs), and six entry-level personnel. The group includes both long-term employees and some new hires. And all twenty-seven members of the team are willing to be part of the evaluation committee to study the results before a decision is made about a complete company rollout."

Describe What's in It for Them

Address the needs of senior management as well as the company. Answer the questions they will be asking, and show them how your recommendation can make them look good. For example, senior management is usually charged with increasing sales and reducing costs. What if this program means saving money by lowering employee turnover yet has a relatively modest cost?

Explain Why This Is a Good Idea Just When
They Are Cutting Unnecessary Spending

"One of our company's key initiatives is to recruit and retain 20 percent more of the best available talent than we did in the last fiscal year. If this training had been in place last year, not only would morale have been higher, but our 23 percent minority associates would have rated their employee satisfaction survey higher. As you remember, for the last three years, our minority associates traditionally rate their satisfaction 3 percent lower than the other population. This training could have helped increase satisfaction and retention. We would lower the cost of recruiting and training new associates."

Explain How This Investment Compares to
Other Investments They Have Already Made

"As a comparison, the initial cost of the pilot for all three offices is 2 percent of what we spend on maintenance agreements for our copier machines in our headquarters building. We will enjoy a great return on investment that many of our other programs do not provide."

Conclude Strong and Clear

"On behalf of the twenty-seven-member committee, thank you for this opportunity. The friendships we have formed and our increased company knowledge is invaluable to us all. The entire team is committed to this project. We are asking for your okay to start the pilot program."

You'll make a strong impression and increase your chances of acceptance when you can be short, clear, and concise. Be prepared and practiced. It's okay to be nervous because nobody sees how you feel. They just see how you look and act.

Using Power Pitching to
Get the Personal Connection Edge

Dozens of factors affect your audience's minds and perceptions whenever and whatever you're teaching, communicating, or selling. You create a competitive edge when you establish a personal connection. You must connect emotionally and intellectually with both individuals and members of an audience so they like you and trust you. They're just like you; if you don't trust the messenger, you don't trust the message.

Power pitching can help you create the personal connection edge you need. Here are some techniques to create your edge.

- **Focus.** It's all about them! If your presentation does not respond to or focus on their concerns or you are too technical for the individuals or audience, they will decide that you don't care about them or their problems. They stand very little chance of seeing the applicability of your message to their problems or needs. Once they get back to work, they won't make your training applicable to their jobs or invest in your solution to their problem. Rather, pick up on their concerns, and address them.

- **Be confident and sincere.** If you appear nervous or unsure, you may seem devious or incompetent.

- **Communicate with your eyes.** Look your listeners right in the eyes long enough to complete a thought or sentence as you talk convincingly about your ideas and information. Avoid darting your eyes about the room because that will not connect or communicate to your listeners.

- **Smile.** Sharing a warm and pleasant smile as you talk will put your audience at ease.

- **Divide and conquer.** Shake hands with everyone — or as many as possible — when they enter the room. Look them in the eyes as you do it and connect with them so you see them as individuals. You'll both feel more comfortable, and you'll become more memorable to them. People are usually shyer with groups of strangers than with one-on-one contacts.

- **Use technology sparingly.** Use technology tools such as PowerPoint to enhance your presentation, not drown it. It can help keep you on track and support your message, but it cannot establish trust. Step out from behind your technology and make yourself the main attraction.

- **Keep it simple and memorable.** What are the three to five key points you want people to remember about the information and you? When your audience debriefs after your presentation or sales conversation, you want them to remember what you said. Therefore, summarize your key talking points into snappy sound bites that are easy to write and remember. Make them interesting and repeatable.

- **Avoid jargon.** Steer clear of overdoing technical language and industry jargon. Rehearse your presentation well in advance with your spouse across the dinner table or with a team member at work. If there is anything they don't understand, you are either not focusing on their interests or you are making it too complicated. Your goal is to be understood and sound conversational as you do it.

- **Tell great success stories.** People learn to resist a sales presentation or go to a meeting with a closed mind, but no one can resist a good story. Use the "Situation, Solution, Success" formula. "Imagine four months from now, you go to work and ..." Paint your listeners a picture of less frustration, more reliability, and cost-effectiveness. Let the person you are communicating with "see" themselves in a different light. And take a lesson from Hollywood — give your stories interesting characters and dialogue plus a dramatic lesson that your prospects can relate to.

- **Rehearse.** The first thirty seconds and the last thirty seconds of your presentation or sales conversation have the most impact. Invest your time to create something original and interesting at the beginning and the end. Then, commit them to memory. Do not shortchange your rehearsals. Three to five rehearsals won't do it. Thirty to fifty rehearsals put you ahead of other speakers or sales professionals, and it will give you even more confidence. Know what you are going to say so well you can forget it!

Here is the bottom line: Everything else being equal, you're way ahead of any other speaker or sales professional when your audience members relate to you, like you, and trust you. Remember, they must first trust you before they can trust the message. Power pitching gives you right conditions in which to earn their trust and gives you the personal connection edge!

The Eleven Biggest Traps to Avoid When You Speak: Turn Dull into Dynamic!

Whenever you open your mouth — whether your audience is one person or a thousand — you want to get a specific message across. Maybe you want your opinions heard at meetings, or perhaps you are giving a formal presentation — internally or externally. Possibly your sales team needs to improve its customer communication, or you're in a position to help your CEO design an important speech.

Anyone who sets out to present, persuade, and propel with the spoken word faces these eleven major pitfalls.

- **Unclear thinking.** If you can't describe what you are talking about in one sentence, you may be guilty of fuzzy focus or trying to cover too many topics. Your listeners will probably be confused too, and their attention will soon wander. Whether you are improving your own skills or helping someone else to create a presentation, the biggest (and most difficult) challenge is to start with a one-sentence premise or objective.

- **No clear structure.** Make it easy for your audience to follow what you are saying. They'll remember it better — and you will too — as you deliver your information and ideas. If you waffle, ramble, or never get to the point, your listeners will tune you out. Start with a strong opening related to your premise; state your premise; and list the rationales or "points of wisdom" that support your premise, supporting each with examples (stories, statistics, metaphors, and case histories). Review what you've covered, take questions if appropriate, and then use a strong close.

- **No memorable stories.** People rarely remember your exact words. Instead, they remember the mental images that your words inspire. Support your key points with vivid, relevant stories. Help your listeners "make the movie" in their heads by using memorable characters, engaging situations, dialogue, suspense, drama, and humor. In fact, if you can open with a highly visual image, dramatic example, or amusing story (but not a joke!) that supports your premise, you'll hook them. Then tie your closing back to your opening scene. They'll never forget it.

- **No emotional connection.** The most powerful communication combines both intellectual and emotional connections. Intellectual connection means appealing to educated self-interest with data and reasoned arguments. Emotional connection comes from engaging the listeners' imaginations. Involve them in your illustrative stories by frequently using the word "you" and by answering their unspoken question, "What's in this for me?" Use what I call a "High I/You Ratio." For example, instead of saying, "I'm going to talk to you about telecommunications," you might say, "You're going to learn the latest trends in telecommunications." Instead of saying, "I want to tell you about Bobby Lewis," consider saying, "Come with me to Oklahoma City. Let me introduce you to my friend, proud father Bobby Lewis." You've pulled the listener into the story.

- **Not speaking to the audience's interests.** As part of one of my sales training seminars, a salesperson role played with me in preparation for a presentation he was about to give that could be worth $20 million to his company. When I asked him about his PowerPoint slides, he admitted he had sixty slides — fifty-eight were about his company and only two about the prospect. After the training, I heard that they reversed the ratio for this and all future presentations based on my advice. Make your presentation about your audience.

- **Wrong level of abstraction.** Are you providing the big picture and overview when your listeners are hungry for details, facts, and specific how-to ideas? Or are you drowning them in data when they need to position themselves with an overview and find out why they should care? Get on the same wavelength with your listeners. My friend, Dr. David Palmer, a Silicon Valley negotiations expert, refers to "fat" and "skinny" words and phrases. Fat words describe the big picture, goals, ideals, and outcomes. Skinny words are minute details and specific who, what, when, and how. In general, senior management needs fat words. Middle management requires medium words — or a combination of both. Technical staff and consumer hotline users are hungry for skinny words. Feed them all according to their appetites. I will discuss fat and skinny words in depth later in the chapter.

- **No pauses.** Good music and good communication both contain changes of pace, pauses, and full rests. This is when listeners think about what has just been said. If you rush on at full speed to crowd in as much information as possible, chances are you've left your listeners back at the station. It's okay to talk quickly, but pause whenever you say something profound or proactive or ask a rhetorical question. This gives the audience a chance to think about what you've said and to internalize it.

- **Irritating non-words.** You know the offenders — hmm, ah, er, you know what I mean. One speaker I heard began each new thought with "Now!" as he scanned his notes to figure out what came next. This might be okay occasionally, but not every thirty seconds. Record yourself to check for similar bad verbal habits. Then keep recording yourself re-delivering the same material until such audience-aggravators have vanished. You could also give your friends permission to point out when you are using these filler words.

- **Stepping on your punch words.** The most important word in a sentence is the punch word. Usually, it's the final word: "Take my wife — PLEASE." But if you drop your voice and then add, "Right?" or "See?!" you've killed the impact of your message. Again, recording yourself will allow you to listen for those instances so you can correct them. Don't sabotage your best shots.

- **Not having a strong opening and closing.** Engage your audience immediately with a powerful, relevant opening with a High I/You Ratio. It can be dramatic, thought-provoking, or even amusing. Hook your listeners immediately with a taste of what is to follow. And never close by asking for questions. Yes, take questions if appropriate, but then go on to deliver your dynamic closing — preferably one that ties back into your opening theme. Last words linger. As with a great musical, you want your audience walking out afterwards humming the tunes.

- **Misusing technology.** Without a doubt, audiovisual tools have added showbiz impact to business and professional speakers' presentations. However, just because it is available, doesn't mean we have to use it! Use technology as a support to your message, not as a crutch. Speakers fall into the trap of overusing or hiding behind their technology. Timid speakers who simply narrate flip chart images, slides, videos, and overheads are rarely passionate and effective. Any visual aid takes the attention away from you. Even the best PowerPoint images will not connect you emotionally — only your personal connection with the audience can do that. Use strong stories instead of technology if at all possible. And never repeat what is on the visuals. If you do, one of you is redundant.

When you can avoid these eleven common pitfalls, you're free to focus on your message and your audience, making you a more dynamic, powerful, and persuasive communicator.

Sound Intelligent, Powerful, Polished, Articulate, and Confident

Do you want to sound intelligent, powerful, polished, articulate, and confident? Of course you do! Try these five techniques.

- **To sound more intelligent:** speak just a bit slower to allow yourself to select your most appropriate vocabulary and to give the impression of thoughtfulness.

- **To sound more powerful:** use short, simple declarative sentences. Say what you mean and mean what you say. Cut out any useless connectors, adjectives, and adverbs (especially superlatives).

- **To sound more polished:** never answer a question with a blunt "yes" or "no." Append a short phrase of clarification. Here are two examples: "No, I did not see it." "Yes, I know Mary."

- **To sound more articulate:** make a special effort to pronounce the final sound in a word and use its energy to carry over to the following word. Pay special attention to final "t" and "ng."

- **To sound more confident:** carry your body up. Hold your head as if you had a crown on it. Don't let your arms and legs swing side-to-side when you move. Keep your elbows and knees close to the midline of your body.

Are You Guilty of the Unconscious Goof That Can Hurt Your Credibility?

You may not have noticed it yet, but once you do, you'll have fun spotting examples everywhere. Some of your friends and associates are guilty. The blight has invaded television, newspapers, and magazines. It crosses all professions and levels of education.

Recently, I counted dozens of examples at a four-day meeting with some of the most brilliant and successful professional speakers and consultants in America. Even YOU may be doing it!

What is this crime against credibility? It's a single, suddenly-popular buzzword that feels like fingernails screeching on a blackboard every time I hear it.

It's "stuff."

Even communication experts are guilty. I maintain that professional speakers, coaches, and consultants are paid for their lifetime of knowledge, innovative ideas, leading-edge strategies, and — most important of all — their eloquence in conveying their ideas across to their audiences.

Yet, I overhear these communicators saying to each other, "The group loved my stuff," or "I gave them my best stuff."

What could be worse? Even worse is, "… and stuff." Some individuals don't seem to know that a period at the end of a sentence is a great way to stop! I've heard, "This will decrease absenteeism and stuff," and "We had a great conversation and stuff."

In Shakespeare's time, "stuff" meant woven cloth, as in, "such stuff as dreams are made on." It has come to mean "miscellaneous," and has even acquired the negative connotation of "junk, debris, or rubbish." Surely, you don't want to clutter your speaking with rubbish?

The worst thing about "stuff" is that it is not specific! My associate, David Palmer, has programmed me to think, "Specificity builds credibility." Each time one of my speaking clients says "stuff," I ask what exactly they mean to say. Some are amazed at how often they use the word — even professionals with PhDs. Yet, their education isn't obvious in their language because of that one useless and irritating word.

Being an Accomplished Speaker

If you're asking yourself what difference it could make, I'll tell you — it makes a huge difference. You get hired because what you say sounds like it is worth paying for. Language that's fuzzy, clumsy, and unclear destroys your credibility and your claim to professionalism. You might as well be delivering your message in "valley-girl" speak, twirling your toe in the rug, and murmuring, "Whatever ..."

Your audience — whether one or a thousand — deserves clear, forceful, and specific language. Toss out meaningless "stuff," and show them what a professional you are.

Levels of Abstraction: Fat and Skinny Words

Nothing can turn your audience or prospect off faster than using fat words when they're hungry for skinny ones or vice versa. I learned this exciting concept from Dr. David Palmer, a Silicon Valley negotiations expert. In his talks on negotiations, he describes "levels of abstraction."

Unless you can match your message to the expectations of your audience — or talk at the same level at which they are listening — you won't connect as well as you would like to. This is true whether your audience is one person or one thousand.

Suppose you write the word "automobile" on a pad — a simple concept. Going up to the next level of abstraction, you could write above it that the car is a "wheeled passenger vehicle," then "surface transportation," then "major force in the world's economy." This process is making the word "automobile" fatter and fatter, larger and larger. These big ideas and abstractions are "fat words." They are great for conveying the big picture, inspiring ideas, and motivating.

Now, let's make the word skinnier. Underneath, you might write "sedan," "Ford sedan," "red four-door Ford sedan." Eventually, you would be talking about a specific car. Those are "skinny" words. They are essential for conveying instructions and solving technical problems. No one who is holding a screwdriver or camera, or who is looking at a blank screen on their computer wants fat words. You'll just frustrate them — maybe make them furious. They want to know minute details and specific who, what, when, and how.

Many of my clients hire me to coach their sales teams. After giving them the automobile illustration, they learn to be more effective by evaluating each other by saying, "Your words are too fat," or "Those words aren't skinny enough." "When you are presenting a sales overview to an executive or senior manager," I ask, "Should your words get fatter or skinnier?"

Upper management needs fat words. After a successful initial interview with an executive, you will be invited to present your offerings to a middle-management team. For this group, your ideas need to be brought down the level of abstraction by using "skinnier words and phrases."

Let's assume you were very effective and persuasive. You made the sale. Now you are dealing with the individuals that make the technology work. That is when the words and phrases need to get skinny — the who, what, how, when, and where do I turn it on?

At what level should you present your information so that you get your message across? It all depends on the audience. You must understand their needs and desires for the information you have to deliver.

As a professional speaker and trainer, I ask my clients, "What do you want the theme of my remarks to be? What is the purpose of the meeting?" For years, I have been hearing, "Get them to sell more," or "Motivate them." My reply would be, "How much are they selling now? How much more?" or "Motivate them to do what?"

Can you see the challenge? Their words are too fat for me to get a clear picture of how to meet and exceed their expectations. With my questioning, I need to drive their comments and expectations down to the level of abstraction by saying things like, "Can you help me understand specifically what you mean by that?" Thank you, David Palmer!

Final Thoughts

There you have it — a one-stop chapter for all the answers you need to make the best sales presentation of your life. Now that you have the information, practice until it becomes true expertise. The best way to reinforce that you know the secrets to a great presentation is to teach somebody else. What are you waiting for?

World Champions' EDGE Testimonial

"I benefited immensely from the conference call tonight. You all did a great job, and I felt it was a good combination of skills. My membership in World Champion's EDGE is one of the best-value investments I've made."

Datta Groover, Ashland, Oregon

World Champions' EDGE Testimonial

 *"Although I have been speaking for many years, the Champions' EDGE continues to give me solid tips and tools every week that I can incorporate in every presentation I make. Their boot camps have helped me kick-start my professional speaking career at an incredibly affordable price. I've done the research and many people pay thousands more for a lot less! The energy, inspiration, and education you will receive from the World Champions' EDGE cannot be found in any other teaching institute. Thanks for all you continue to do for me!"*

Russ Dantu, Speaker, Trainer, Author, Coach
Calgary, Alberta, Canada

CHAPTER 19
When You're in Speaking, You're in Sales

by Craig Valentine

When you are in the speaking business, you are in sales. Speakers have to sell their message or their audience will not take action, and they will not make any kind of difference in the lives of their audience members. Knowing this, it is amazing how many speakers never study the essential art of selling.

You will profit immensely from what you're about to read. Why? Because at the end of this lesson, you'll find the titles of three books on selling that will put you ahead of 99 percent of people who ever tried to sell anything — message, product, or service.

You will pick up four specific tools along with a special formula you can use to easily sell anything from your message to your products to your services. Oh, wait a minute. There was a tool right there. Did you see it?

Tool 1: Fix Your Focus

Here is the tool you probably did not see. Most speakers would have said, "I am going to share with you some tools and a formula you can use to [blah blah blah]." Guess what? Nobody cares what *you* are going to share. We care about what *we* are going to get, so here is a wise rule to follow. During your speech, if you find yourself saying, "I am going to share ..." say instead, "You are going to receive ..." or "You are going to pick up ..." It is a small change that makes a huge difference to your audience members.

In our Champion's EDGE coaching sessions, we call it "The You Turn." It happens when your speaking persona wisely replaces the "I" focus with the "you" focus. It places the emphasis on the audience.

A wonderful whet-the-appetite statement is always, "In the next forty-five minutes, you will gain ..." For example, "In the next forty-five minutes, you will discover the tools the top managers use to get more work done through others. Believe it or not, you will be able to get more done in one hour than most managers can get done in an entire day. And — here's the best part — you'll do it with much less stress!" That is a correctly fixed "you" focus.

Tool 2: Find Their Pain

Letting your audience know how they will benefit from your message isn't enough. You must also understand where they hurt and why. In other words, you must find their pain. And once you find their pain, what should you do next? Should you immediately offer them some solutions? No!

Instead, you should increase their pain. I know this sounds cruel, but let's face the following reality: some people don't move until it gets too uncomfortable to stand still.

When I presented at the MIT Sloan Sales Conference, I heard one of the sales speakers describe this process as finding the pain and twisting the knife. We need to agitate our audiences to the point where they think, "Okay, please give me some solutions." When they are thirsty for a cure, they will gladly accept and embrace your message. Believe me, they will thank you for it.

When you give them the solution before pushing them to their pain threshold, they still have the strength to resist making a change. And we know that everybody resists change. Our job as a speaker is to make our audience members face their own disturbing reality so that they want — and feel the need — to break through their own inertia to strive for remarkable results.

Tool 3: Don't Sell the Product, Sell the Result

I once heard real estate and information marketing guru Ron LeGrand say, "People don't buy paint, they buy beautiful walls." The legendary direct marketing genius Joseph Sugarman said, "Don't sell the drill, sell the hole." Speakers can adapt this to "Don't sell the process, sell the result." This came into play years ago when I bought my first car.

I was on a car lot looking at Eagle Talons when a salesperson approached me and said, "This car is fantastic. It has anti-lock brakes, automatic windows, and easy steering." In other words, he was trying to sell me the car by highlighting the product's features. I didn't understand at the time why I didn't feel convinced and left that dealership without purchasing. In other words, he was trying to sell me the car instead of the results. I didn't know why at the time, but I didn't feel convinced, so I left that dealership without purchasing.

Later that day, I visited another car lot and looked at a similar Eagle Talon. The salesperson must have assessed me (young, hip, and driven by testosterone) before he approached me. He asked, "You're looking at that car?" I said, "Yes." He said, "You're going to look great in it. You'll be whizzing down the road pumping your music, and the girls will be all over you!" I immediately asked, "Where do I sign?"

The second salesperson succeeded because he sold me results whereas the first salesperson tried to sell me a car. Because of this new salesperson, I already felt myself driving down the highway with several raving female fans. He sold me the result I wanted to hear. And you know what? He lied! Don't sell the product (or the process). Sell the result.

Tool 4: Transition from an I-Focused Story to a You-Focused Message

When selling your message to your audience, transition smoothly from your I-focused story to your you-focused message. Telling an I-focused story — one that you tell in the first-person — creates a connection between you and your audience. However, when you are ready to make your point, it's time to make it about your audience by making the transition to a you-focused message.

For example, when I finish telling my I-focused story about facing the reality that I was out of shape and overweight, I can easily transition into the following kind of you-focused message:

> "… so that scale was my reality, and it prompted me to change. Reality hurts, but the most important thing you must do as a leader is to get your people to face their reality. If you don't, they will never change. When you do, you're already halfway to your new vision."

Do you see how I moved from talking about my situation to focusing on them and the message they should take? That's how you can begin driving your point home. *The more you use "you," the more they hear you.*

Craig's Special EDGE Sales Formula

You now have four specific tools to help you sell:

- Fix your focus on your audience.
- Find — and increase — their pain.
- Sell the benefit — what they'll get, not what they'll buy.
- Transition your message to their needs and realities.

Armed with those four specific tools to help you sell, let's dive into a special formula — the EDGE formula — for making sure you reach and motivate everyone in the room.

Selling results is key to motivating people. You can divide results into four categories. If you intentionally offer results from each one of these categories during your speech, you will motivate the vast majority of your audience. All of the results answer the famous question: WIIFM (What's In It for Me)?

- E = Esteem More
- D = Do More
- G = Gain More
- E = Enjoy More

Esteem More

A result that helps you *esteem more* is prestigious. For example, you might tell a group of leaders: "When you put this process to use, you will become known as the kind of leader others admire and want to follow."

Do More

A result that helps you *do more* is empowering. For example, you might tell a group of managers: "As soon as you start integrating this four-step delegation process, you will find yourself getting more done in one hour than you used to get done in one day, and you won't need any additional resources."

Gain More

A result that helps you *gain more* is profitable. For example, you might tell a group of entrepreneurs: "You'll be able to generate more leads, customers, and profits with a one-hour speech than most business owners can get with an entire month of frustrating efforts."

Enjoy More

A result that helps you *enjoy more* is fun. You might tell a group of teachers: "When you follow these Four Rs to Remarkable results, you will feel the stress fall off your shoulders as a new vitality surges through you."

In the "you" focus of my speech for the World Championship of Public Speaking, I said the following:

> "Taking five minutes of silence each day will give you confidence exuding from every pore of your being. Five minutes of silence will grant you a peacefulness, a tranquility, a serenity that you never even knew existed. And five minutes of silence will sooner or later lead you to feel fulfilled."

The confidence is related to the *do more* result. The peacefulness, tranquility, serenity, and fulfillment are all related to the *enjoy more* result. In my speeches now (usually thirty to sixty minutes long), I make sure I offer results from all four categories across the EDGE board. That is your key to selling success.

Someone who is not motivated by financial gain will probably be motivated by more recognition. If he's not motivated by recognition, chances are he wants less stress, more freedom, or at least more enjoyment out of his job or life. Check your message against the EDGE formula and make sure you offer results from each category. If you do, you will see motivated people who can't wait to leave their seats and take on the world.

Final Thoughts

You're waiting for that list of books, aren't you? Well, that's because I used another powerful sales tool at the beginning of this lesson. A very powerful sales tool is the *promise* — I promised to reveal something later on. When you do that in your presentation, people will stay alert to find it.

Well, since I promised them to you, here they are. These are the books that will make a great difference in your personal and professional life. After all, as soon as you wake up in the morning, no matter what you do in life, you will have to sell something. Mastering this one skill will do wonders for your future.

Books

- *Triggers* by Joseph Sugarman (advertising copy genius)
- *The Psychology of Persuasion* by Kevin Hogan (genius on influence)
- *Soft Selling in a Hard World* by Richard Vass

There are your keys to successful speaking — have a "you" focus, take your audience to the EDGE, and promote results instead of products. Happy selling!

World Champions' EDGE Testimonial

 *"Together with the ongoing EDGE program, you truly are my professional speaking mastermind group. My first paid speaking engagement is scheduled in two weeks! I cannot thank each of you enough for the encouragement and support you have given me."*

Kevin Spalding, Gastonia, North Carolina

World Champions' EDGE Testimonial

"Since your teleseminar, I have picked up three speaking jobs (all paid) with several others to be determined soon. Thanks for all you've done."

Dan Weedin, Poulsbo, Washington

CHAPTER 20
What Does a Master Do Differently?
Seven Essential Habits of Master Presenters

by Darren LaCroix

What do you notice that people who are truly "masters" on stage have in common? What are those subtle differences that over time put in motion large differences that separate them from the pack? As a student of presentation skills since 1992, I have some definite observations. It just gets clearer as time goes on. Though they are simple habits, over time they define our growth rate. Do you incorporate these seven essential habits?

Habit 1: Think Differently

The first thing Craig Valentine did when he got off the plane after winning the World Championship of Public Speaking was to get a book on public speaking. That is the attitude of a true master presenter. People who are the best and have a passion for their craft and their message are always looking to learn more. If every presenter had Craig's attitude, rarely would anyone ever sit through a boring presentation again.

When I jumped into the comedy world, I took every class I could. Many of my teachers became life-changing mentors. I've invested $10,000 each year for the past three years in my own education. Since that has been so helpful, I have already invested over $20,000 for next year. Will you invest more in your own self-development next year?

Habit 2: Effort in Their Introduction

A master presenter understands that "setting up" the listener is just as important as what is said. Too many presenters do not put any time or effort into their introduction. If anything, they give the introducer an ego-filled bio that is usually about seven minutes too long. True professionals keep their introductions under three minutes. Their introductions have "you-focused" questions in them. These are followed by your credibility, and then a single humbling piece of personal information. The introduction should answer the question "Why should people listen to you? What will they get out of giving you their time?"

Habit 3: Focus on Connecting with the Audience First

Master presenters are fully aware that they must connect with an audience before they can persuade them. The connection is crucial. This is why I spend a great deal of time researching my keynote audiences beforehand. I don't stop there either. I will also attend other sessions prior to mine just to find that one "nugget" that will allow me to connect with audience members. In fact, this ties into the previous point — part of your introduction's purpose is to start the process of connecting. Do you strategically focus on connecting?

Habit 4: Provide Adequate Pauses

Pauses are for the audience's benefit, not their own comfort level. Too many speakers only pause long enough for their own comfort. They do not hold the pause long enough for the audience to "think." This is the whole point of the presentation. Master presenters know that if they are not letting them reflect on their perspective, they are in fact breaking the connection with the audience. All too often, the presenter is the problem; not the audience. If you ask a simple yes-or-no question, a short pause is plenty. If your question requires deeper thought, pause long enough for the audience to think about it! Do you pause long enough? If they are not reflecting, you are not connecting!

Habit 5: Worry Bigger

Master presenters are much more concerned for the audience's outcome, rather than what the audience will think of them. I recently interviewed Maria Austin, a professional trainer, for an audio learning program for new trainers. She is one of the best trainers I know. She has what I call the "Maria Mindset." Before she was a trainer, she was in customer service. She brought her "serious service" attitude to her training. She looks at both professions in exactly the same way. The only difference is that her product is now education. She is adamant about what the audience members take away. She fully understands that it is not about her.

Habit 6: Get Lots of Laughs

You don't have to use humor in presentations — unless, of course, you want the audience to listen. Although you can have a powerful presentation without it, most master presenters usually have heavy doses of humor. Here is a crucial difference between good speakers and masters: master presenters infuse the humor into the story. It is not a tangent from the message.

Many less-experienced presenters will tell a joke or use something they found on the Internet. They use it to break the ice. Wrong! Humor should always have some relevance to your main message. Otherwise, it is a detour and wastes valuable time! Keep in mind what comic Steve Allen said: "Humor arises between the incongruity between the character and the situation." It is the essence of the "sitcom." For speakers, we need "sit-stories." The purpose of the story should be to anchor a key point. If you are not getting laughs now, learn to anchor your points with stories.

Habit 7: Crave Feedback

When master presenters walk off the platform, they are fully aware that a crucial part of their next presentation is just about to begin. It does not matter what we say, it only matters what the audience hears. Presenters who are passionate about their message are constantly evolving. They are constantly testing new ideas. Things that are common in my keynotes now originated as experiments. For example, I never used to show a video clip of my very first time on stage. I also never used to show a photo of my closet full of video recordings. They are now essential to my keynotes, but they may someday be replaced with something more powerful. For instance, when I spoke in Canada recently, I had a video introduce me!

Final Thoughts

Are you on track to become a master presenter if you are not already? If you believe you already are, may I suggest you read the first essential habit again? I get off track occasionally myself, but it only takes one humbling audience to remind us we all still have much to learn. Where will your current habits take you in five years?

What Does a Master Do Differently?

The Experts Behind
Speaker's EDGE

A t the time of this printing, the experts collectively bring a total of seventy-three years of experience. With that kind of experience and expertise, you can only increase your learning curve on your road to becoming a great speaker.

Mark Brown

Nationally acclaimed speaker Mark Brown has dedicated his career to delivering uplifting messages to people all over the world. With his "tell it like it is" approach, he challenges some of the most serious issues facing schools today. He uses a unique combination of humor and poignancy to reach the most diverse audiences, and he is committed to continually inspiring people from all walks of life.

Originally from Kingston, Jamaica, Mark immigrated to the United States at age eighteen with $40 in his pocket and a dream of a better life. He never imagined he'd devote his life to helping others. He spent fifteen years working in the banking and direct marketing industries as a computer analyst before choosing to develop his public speaking skills. After recovering from a life-threatening illness in the summer of 1993, he made a commitment to excel as a communicator. His commitment earned him a 1995 Harlem YMCA Black Achievers in Industry Award. His efforts were further rewarded when he became Toastmasters International's 1995 World Champion of Public Speaking.

Mark, a member of the National Speakers Association, is the recipient of a 1996 Music Service Award from the National Association of Negro Musicians. He has been the subject of articles in several publications, including the *San Diego Union-Tribune* and the *New York Times*. He has also been featured in print and broadcast media in Hong Kong, the Middle East, the United States, Canada, and the Caribbean. In 1999, The National Academy of Television Arts and Sciences nominated his presentation in the Maine PBS television special *Words Count with Mark Brown* for an Emmy Award for Outstanding Educational/Instructional Program.

Mark makes over 200 presentations each year at conferences, school assemblies, symposiums, conventions, and corporate meetings. He is in high demand by adult and youth audiences throughout North America.

His purpose is threefold: to touch your head and make you think; to touch your heart and make you feel; and to touch your hands and make you act.

Patricia Fripp, CSP, CPAE

"Fripp is the most reliable, versatile, easy-to-work-with, hassle-free, customer-friendly speaker we've ever booked," says Dan Maddux, Executive Director of the American Payroll Association.

Patricia Fripp, CSP, CPAE is an award-winning speaker, author, sales presentation trainer, and in-demand speech coach. Her speech-coaching clients include corporate leaders, celebrity speakers, well-known sports and media personalities, ministers, and sales teams. *Meetings and Conventions* magazine named her "One of the Ten Most Electrifying Speakers in North America." She delivers high-energy, high-content, and dramatically memorable presentations. Steven Covey's *Executive Excellence* magazine calls her "One of the Top Fifty Consultants, Trainers, Speakers, Authors, and Professors Who Cover the Seven Dimensions of Excellence." Kiplinger's Personal Finance named her speaking school the sixth best way to invest one thousand dollars in your career.

Before becoming a full-time speaker, Patricia enjoyed a successful twenty-four-year career in a service industry. She owned two highly successful businesses and trained both service and sales personnel. Her first paid speaking engagements and training seminars began in 1976.

Since 1980, she has spoken to over 100 groups every year — many of them repeat engagements. This includes Fortune 100 companies and major associations worldwide. The National Speakers Association, with more than 4,000 members, elected her their first female president in 1984. She has won or been awarded every designation given by NSA, including their Hall of Fame and their highest honor, the Cavett Award, considered the "Oscar" of the speaking world.

Patricia is the author of two books, *Get What You Want!* and *Make It, So You Don't Have to Fake It!,* and the coauthor of *Speaking Secrets of the Masters* and *Insights into Excellence.* She is featured in the *Bulletproof Manager* video series which is sold in over fifty countries. Fripp starred in the popular training film *Travel the Road to Success: An Adventure in Customer Service.*

Fripp's hobby of avid movie going and attending screen-writing seminars adds extra pizzazz to her training sessions that is not generally found with other speech coaches. A media star herself, she has been featured in the press and on TV for over thirty years.

Patricia keeps good company, and is a founding faculty member of MentorU.com, a distance learning company of world-class business experts providing training utilizing the latest Internet technologies. She is a member of the prestigious Speakers Roundtable, consisting of twenty-two of the most successful, in-demand speakers in the country.

Darren LaCroix

In 2001, Darren LaCroix, outspoke 25,000 contestants from fourteen countries to win the title of World Champion of Public Speaking. That was just a benchmark. Since that victory, Darren has traveled the world demystifying the process of creating a powerful speech. He has roused audiences in faraway places like Saudi Arabia, China, Oman, Malaysia, and Taiwan with his inspirational journey from first-rate chump to first-class champ, proving anything is possible if you are willing to work for it.

Darren may have been "born without a funny bone in my body," but he possessed the desire to learn and the willingness to fail necessary to achieve his dream. The self-proclaimed "student of comedy" is living proof that humor is a skill that can be learned.

As a keynote speaker since 1994, he brings his incredible story to conferences around the world. He is consistently the top-rated speaker at conferences. He changes the way people think about challenges, humor, and presentations forever. His clients include IBM, Fidelity Investments, and numerous associations too long to list!

He is known as the person who helps speakers launch their careers in professional speaking. His trademarked program *Get Paid to Speak by Next Week®* has helped many speakers earn their very first checks. He also supports speakers doing business coaching through his Internet program *Get Paid to Speak TV.*

Now Darren is in high demand as a speaker coach. The new standard for advanced presentation skills was created when he co-created *How Professional Presenters Can Own the Stage.* There is no other program on the market that even comes close to this transformational program. Viewers witness exactly how coaches can create lasting significant improvement in just two days.

His successful book, *Laugh & Get Rich: How to Profit from Humor in Any Business* is in its sixth printing. It contains interviews with corporate executives who share his philosophy. Now translated into three languages, it is a mainstay on business bookshelves.

As cofounder of The Humor Institute and a cocreator of *The Humor Boot Camp®*, Darren directs seminars that help presenters wisely use the power of humor to lighten up their presentations. He is also the award-winning producer of the film *Healing, Hope, and Humor.*

Ed Tate, CSP

Using the principles he continues to teach today, Ed Tate won the coveted Toastmasters International 2000 World Championship of Public Speaking. To date, he has spoken professionally in forty-six states, twelve countries, and on five continents. This internationally known keynote speaker has earned a reputation as the "speaker who energizes, educates, and entertains."

Ed is also a successful trainer and author. As a trainer, Ed worked with CareerTrack (the largest public seminar company at the time) where he was frequently booked for 100 presentations a year. Following CareerTrack, he became the training executive for the *Denver Rocky Mountain News* where he established the company's training department. There, he created twenty-seven programs and trained more than 1,100 employees annually. In 2001, he led the transition team that merged the 145-year-old *Rocky* with its 125-year-old rival, *The Denver Post*, in a merger that involved more than 5,000 people.

As an author, Ed cowrote the book *Motivational Selling: Advice on Selling Effectively, Staying Motivated, and Being a Peak Sales Producer.* He's also contributed to *Stories Trainers Tell* and *The Seven Strategies of Master Presenters*. Additionally, Ed coproduced the CD audio programs *Speaking Secrets of the Champions* and *Connect with Any Audience*.

His clients enjoy his unique ability to tailor presentations to their organization's requirements.

Ed's success in business has spanned more than two decades. For fourteen years, he was a successful national account executive selling over $500 million in products and services to corporations and entrepreneurs throughout the United States. He cocreated two business units that produced more than $1.25 billion in revenue.

Since 1998, Ed has been principal of Ed Tate & Associates, LLC, a professional development firm. Besides keynote and endnote presentations and workshops, he delivers in-person and do-it-yourself tools and expertise on leadership, executive communication skills, coping with change, team building, and sales presentation skills.

Craig Valentine, MBA

Craig Valentine is the president of The Communication Factory, LLC, an award-winning company that helps organizations embrace change.

Craig has traveled the world helping hundreds of organizations reap the profitable rewards that come from embracing change. A motivational speaker, he has spoken around the world giving as many as 160 presentations per year. In 1999, he was named the Toastmasters International World Champion of Public Speaking. Craig has used his Four-Step Change Formula to:

- Win Salesperson of the Year three times for Glencoe/McGraw-Hill's Mid-Atlantic Division
- Become a top-rated, award-winning management trainer for one of the most prestigious and largest seminar companies in the United States
- Produce sales years of 233 percent, 157 percent, and 152 percent of goal for McGraw-Hill
- Sell more than $8 million in educational resources in a single year
- Win Events Manager of the Year for the National Small Business Council, Inc.
- Win a Congressional Achievement Award from the United States Congress for excellence in communications
- Earn the Distinguished Alumni Award from Johns Hopkins University
- Receive hundreds of speaking awards
- Help the United Way of Central Maryland reach its $45 million fund-raising goal in 2000 by training their loaned executives

Craig Valentine is also the cofounder of the World Champions' EDGE program, which helps up-and-coming speakers turn their presentations into huge profits. Valentine is the author of the ground-breaking book, The *Nuts and Bolts of Public Speaking,* coauthor of the book, *World Class Speaking,* and contributing author for the book *Guerrilla Marketing on the Front Lines.* He has an MBA from Johns Hopkins University, and he is certified as a Co-Active Coach and a Guerrilla Marketing Coach. He is the coleader of the Guerrilla Marketing Coach Certification Program, and he is a recognized expert in the Master Business Building Club.

ABOUT THE HONORS
Professional Designations and Awards

All the authors have been honored with professional designations and awards given by a jury of their peers. Not just a simple set of words and letters, they are proof of their ability to practice their craft and teach others.

Toastmasters International
World Championship of Public Speaking

What does it mean to be a World Champion of Public Speaking? Each year, more than 25,000 Toastmasters members begin a quest to be the best in an international competition sponsored by Toastmasters International, the world's premier organization devoted to helping people develop their speaking, listening, and leadership skills.

In the end, one person triumphs, standing alone as the World Champion of Public Speaking. Once you have been crowned the World Champion of Public Speaking, you are not allowed to compete in this competition again. This encourages them to then teach what they have learned from this intense competition.

Four of the speaker coaches represented on this book have each earned this rare and prestigious title. In addition to that, they have also coached many winners and finalists from around the world in this speech competition.

Cavett Award

The Cavett Award is the highest honor NSA bestows on its members. It is presented annually to a professional speaker whose accomplishments over the years have reflected outstanding credit, respect, honor, and admiration in NSA and the speaking profession. The award is named after NSA's late founder, Cavett Robert, CSP, CPAE, whose illustrious career helped guide and inspire many NSA members.

CSP

The Certified Speaking Professional (CSP) designation, conferred by the National Speakers Association and the International Federation for Professional Speakers, is the speaking profession's international measure of professional platform skill.

The CSP designation is earned through demonstrating competence in a combination of standards:
- Professional platform skills
- Professional business management
- Professional education
- Professional association

CPAE Hall of Fame

Established in 1977, the Council of Peers Award for Excellence (CPAE) is a lifetime award for speaking excellence and professionalism given to speakers who have been evaluated by their peers and judged to have mastered seven categories:
- Material
- Style
- Experience
- Delivery
- Image
- Professionalism
- Communication

The award is not based on celebrity status, number of speeches, amount of income, or involvement in NSA.

Learn More about World Champions' EDGE

D id you get some new ideas out of this book? What if you had regular access to five of the best speaker coaches in the world? What if they could provide you with the answers to your presentation questions? What would that be worth?

Want to make the most valuable $1 investment of your life? **Go to www.WorldChampionsEDGE.com.**

Get access to Hall of Fame Speaker, Patricia Fripp, CSP, CPAE, and World Champions of Public Speaking Mark Brown (1995), Craig Valentine (1999), Ed Tate (2000), and Darren LaCroix (2001)!

Your $1 will get you thirty days of instant access to:

- Over 170 audio lessons on virtually every speaking subject

- Two sixty-minute EDGEucational CDs that you'll receive right away

- Over forty *Ask the Champs* conference call MP3s (now featuring live speaker coaching)

- Online access to EDGEnet where you can connect with serious fellow speakers around the world

- Twenty-percent discount on all of our resources, Champ Camps, and speaker's conferences!

- Free pass to the biannual EDGE Summit
  — a one-day, all-access session where members set the agenda!

You will also get $319.95 in free bonuses when you join the EDGE (you can keep these no matter what!)

Why would we give you access to all that for just $1? We are not crazy! We know you will get so much value that you will stick with the EDGE program for years to come. We are willing to prove our value for just a small investment!

Join Patricia Fripp, Mark Brown, Craig Valentine, Ed Tate, and Darren LaCroix!

How much proof do you need for $1?

Go to www.WorldChampionsEDGE.com and get thirty days of the EDGE for $1!

Notes and EDGE Ideas

Notes and EDGE Ideas

Notes and EDGE Ideas

Two Ways to Order

Online   Order online at www.WorldChampionResources.com

Postal Mail   Send your completed order form to
World Champions' EDGE
7582 Las Vegas Blvd. S. #144
Las Vegas, NV 89123

Professional Development Tools

Speaker's EDGE: Secrets and Strategies   Paperback, 158 pages
for Connecting with Any Audience   _____ x \$15.00 = _____

Please add 8.1% sales tax for orders shipped to Nevada addresses.

Shipping and Handling

USA: Add \$5 for the first book and \$1 for each additional book.
International: \$9 for the first book; \$5 for each additional book.

Payment

❐ Check   Credit Card: ❐ Visa ❐ MC ❐ Amex

Card Number _____

Name on Card _____

Exp. Date_____ CSV# (on back of card) _____

Signature _____

Your Information

Name _____

Address _____

City_____ State _____ Zip _____

Telephone _____

E-mail Address_____